WHOSE À LA CARTE MENU?

Angela Hanley

Whose à la Carte Menu?
Exploring Catholic Themes in Context

the columba press

First published in 2014 by
the columba press
55A Spruce Avenue,
Stillorgan Industrial Park,
Blackrock, Co. Dublin

Cover design by David Mc Namara CSsR
Cover image of the National University of Ireland, Maynooth courtesy
of Prof. Salvador Ryan
Origination by The Columba Press
Printed in Ireland by SPRINT-Print Ltd

ISBN 978 1 78218 176 7

For Patrick, Dominic and the babe yet to be born

Acknowledgements

My grateful thanks to those people who encouraged this project from its inception – to Gearoid, my husband, sounding board, listener of moans, supplier of books; to my children, Carey and Colman, from whom I learned the most valuable of life's lessons. To Pauline Brophy who told me to 'just DO it!' and who, along with Levina Reeves and Martin Hanley were perceptive and challenging readers of the text as it grew. To Sean O Boyle, Columba Press, who knew the book was in there somewhere almost before I knew it myself. To Philip Gleeson OP, who generously shared books and good humour. To Joe Kavanagh OP, the Irish Dominican Province and the Priory Institute, without whom I would not have a voice.

Contents

Introduction   11

CHAPTER ONE In the Beginning   15

CHAPTER TWO Church: A Building or a People?   25

CHAPTER THREE Tradition: As it was in the beginning,
                    is now and ever shall be ...   33

CHAPTER FOUR Doctrine and Dogma   43

CHAPTER FIVE The Papacy   53

CHAPTER SIX Councils: Twenty-One and Counting   61

CHAPTER SEVEN Infallibility   71

CHAPTER EIGHT Modernism   79

CHAPTER NINE The Second Vatican Council   89

CHAPTER TEN Birth Control   101

CHAPTER ELEVEN Canon Law   119

CHAPTER TWELVE Fundamentalism   129

CHAPTER THIRTEEN Translation of the Missal   139

CHAPTER FOURTEEN Priesthood   151

CHAPTER FIFTEEN Sexual Abuse in Church   161

EPILOGUE Here I Stand   173

Bibliography   193

Introduction

For a number of years the phrase 'à la carte Catholic' became a very popular term used disparagingly by some leaders within the Catholic Church. They used it when various church teachings came under scrutiny or were challenged by members of the church. In the United States, the phrase they used was 'cafeteria Catholic'. Any dissenting voice could be dismissed by use of this term. It was also taken up quite enthusiastically by others in the wider church who believed that there was only one way to be Catholic. Those leaders and followers, who used the phrase with such disdain, failed to understand that the term 'à la carte Catholic' could also be justifiably applied to them – for they, too, were selecting the bits that suited their purposes. Just as there is more than one way to be Irish, there is more than one way to be Catholic. Human beings are meaning-making creatures that live in community and are influenced by these relationships and by the larger story of their culture. So, it is not a question of whether a person is an à la carte Catholic or not. The question is: whose menu is being selected and followed?

This is an important question because there are two very distinct worldviews in Catholic theology that define and influence everything else that flows from them. One worldview is called 'classicist' and the other is 'historical consciousness'. In a nutshell, classicist thinking uses deductive reasoning and emphasises the static, the immutable, the eternal and the unchanging. Historical consciousness uses inductive reasoning and emphasises the changing, the developing, evolving and historical; it allows for the possibility of growth and change through the acquisition of new knowledge, insights and experience. Because they are two fundamentally different ways of thinking, there is rarely any overlap. In many ways, it is as if they are two different languages. This inevitably leads to extended debates about what is right and wrong without any useful resolution of issues for the church at large. The birth control issue is a perfect example of the debate between classicist and historical consciousness thinking. The classicist thinking prevailed at the time, but did not succeed in the long run, as people have obviously come to their own conclusions about the rights and wrongs of birth control.

'Knowledge is power' is a well-known, often-quoted phrase. It is usually spoken of in positive terms – the gaining and keeping of knowledge. This book grew from looking at this phrase from the other end, so to speak – the lack of knowledge as powerlessness. As I tried to apply the lessons of experience to my faith, I began to see that there was a growing gap between the truth of my life and my attempts to live my faith within the structure of the Catholic Church. I did not know how to address this gap, mainly because I did not have the knowledge that was necessary to do so.

I was fortunate that I got the opportunity to study theology. This gave me the knowledge and vocabulary I needed to articulate an adult faith rooted in the reality of my life. My faith is a real and living thing. It is not an add-on. It is not a duty to be performed. It is rooted in who I am as a person in my journey to this point in my life. It is the light and guide to the person I want to be as I grow in age, knowledge and experience. Part of my faith journey is sharing my theological experience with those who are happy to listen. Over time, I discovered a genuine interest in some of the thoughts and insights that I shared. This interest came from a broad spectrum of people. It included those who were reared in the Catholic faith, but life and experience turned them away from it and, in some cases, made them quite hostile to it; it included those who are still formally practising within the current church structures; it included those who still are people of faith, but find that they are alienated and marginalised – that the church no longer makes sense to them. This is a large and ever-growing group.

The idea for this book grew out of these theological conversations with people who never had the opportunity to learn much about church. I began to hear the question 'why has nobody told us this before?' more frequently. As much as I tried to ignore the question, it kept returning to me, until, like a stone in my shoe, I could ignore it no longer. My purpose in writing this book is to take a number of themes familiar to Catholics, but about which, they have been told very little. I attempt to explain them in clear and straightforward language, avoiding theological jargon and technical theological concepts, but I hope, never in a patronising way. The choice of subjects is eclectic, but has a kind of logic that I hope will be obvious as the reader follows through. I have used reliable and respected sources for the information, and, to my knowledge, I have used them fairly.

Given that my own faith has been the springboard for this book, I have included a personal essay. I have included this to make it abundantly clear where I stand. The more I come alive to my faith the less connection I feel to what should be my community of faith. This strikes me as an extraordinary dissonance. It is indeed a clanging cymbal. But this is where I find myself: the more my faith in the risen Christ takes hold of me, the less hospitable I find the church as a place to practice. So, even though it was not my intention to include such an essay when planning the book, it seems that my own story is a necessary part. It is deliberately placed at the end, so that the reader may read it or ignore as she or he chooses.

Even though scholars now accept that reformer Martin Luther did not actually declaim the following, it still sounds good to me! 'Here I stand, I can do no other.'

Chapter One

In the Beginning

To begin any journey, we can only begin from where we stand. Part of knowing how to go forward with some hope of success is to have some sense of how we got to where we are. Only then can we hope to benefit from the best of our experiences and learn from the worst. This is true of the affairs of the nation, as well as true of one-on-one relationships of marriage, partnership and friendship. It is also true of faith communities. No person is perfect, no group of people is perfect. Therefore, no organisation comprised of people can ever be perfect. The most that can be hoped is that it will be as good as possible in the circumstances in which it finds itself. This is as true of the Christian Church as it is of any other community of rela-tionships, big or small. It behoves every Christian to be mindful of this, especially since for a good part of its history, the Catholic Church regarded itself as the 'perfect society'. Believing oneself to be perfect, even corporately, opens the door to arrogance, pride and what can only be called a god-complex. It is a very short journey from believing one possesses something of God, to believing one possesses God.

In the Creed we profess to believe in 'the one, holy, catholic and apostolic Church'. It should be noted that the 'catholic' in this instance is spelt with a small 'c'. This 'catholic' means to be universal and broad-based. Unfortunately, Catholic, with a capital 'C' does not foster quite the same idea of universality, despite its global spread. It is not all that long ago, certainly within living memory for many people, that the phrase 'outside the Church, no salvation' was commonplace – again, the short journey from possessing something of God, to possessing God.

Christian theology evolved as early Christians explored the meaning of God as revealed by Jesus. They tried to define who and what they understood Jesus to be. Then, in the light of this understanding, how best to respond to God. In Christianity, theology has a distinct air of mystique about it because of the obvious God connection but this is a misplaced notion. Theology (from the Greek *theos,* meaning 'god', and *logia,* meaning 'study of, or discourse about, something') is really little more than speculation or, to put it more bluntly, best guess. High quality guess work, certainly, carried out by some of the most astonishingly able minds over hundreds of years. Yet when all is pared away to the core, it still remains best guess. This is not as shocking as it might seem, because there is nothing particularly wrong with such activity. It is simply the use of our ability to reason to try to understand and interpret particular events in the light of our existing knowledge and experience. The problems arise when those involved in the speculation begin to forget that it *is* just best guess and start applying the properties of certainty or infallibility to it – the short journey from possessing something of God, to possessing God.

Who Jesus was, and what his purpose for humanity was, is so clear to Christians today it is difficult to believe that there was a time Christians had to figure it all out for themselves. Jesus did not leave a complete set of instructions for his followers to slavishly follow to the letter. He left general principles that, if followed with any degree of consistency, would make life more tolerable for all who profess to follow him. His testimony was how he lived his life. And this is where the interpretation begins.

Jesus left no written texts. He spread his message by interacting with people as and where he found them. The people heard his words according to their understanding and their needs. It was not until twenty years after his death and resurrection that the first writings about Jesus appeared. These came from Paul of Tarsus from the early fifties to late sixties CE. This is when the interpretation began. Not all letters attributed to St Paul were written by him. Of the thirteen letters with Paul's name, only seven are considered to be from his hand. The other six were written by people closely associated with Paul and who, as was the practice for the time, used his name to lend the letters authority. Paul's writings have very little of the story of Jesus of Nazareth in them. He focuses on the reality of the risen Christ and what that calls forth in us as followers of Christ, both in our attitudes and behaviour. For the Jesus that ate and drank, laughed and cried, we need to look to the gospels.

The gospels, like Paul's letters, were written down many years after Jesus' death. They were not direct reportage by someone following Jesus around. They were written to fulfil a particular theological need of the groups from which they grew. They were produced in the order of: Mark (66–70 CE), Matthew and Luke (80–90 CE) and John (90–100 CE). Nothing is known about the individual authors, although there is speculation that Luke was possibly a physician. The dates are assumed because of some of the internal information in the gospels themselves. Christianity (though it was not called such at this time) was a sect within Judaism. Its members were allowed to participate in the synagogue as well as having its own worship separate from it. This is not surprising because the initial followers were Jewish, just as Jesus was Jewish. Such pluralism was not unusual. There were many groups within Judaism: Pharisees, Sadducees, Essenes, disciples of John the Baptist, to name a few. To understand the reason for the appearance of the gospels, we need to have some idea of what was happening politically at this time.

From the early part of the first century, there was a group within the Jewish population (the Zealots) that wanted to challenge the power of Rome and establish Israel's independence from the Roman empire. The heavy taxes that the Roman governors could impose at will were a source of contention. However, when the authorities began to take a hand in appointing the high priest from among the

Jews, the clash with Rome was inevitable. The high priest had the significant role of representing the Jewish people before God at all the important sacred events. Increasingly, they were hand-picked from among Jews sympathetic to Rome. Eventually, in 66–70 CE, there was a revolt by the Jews against the Romans. This resulted in many deaths at the hands of the Romans in Galilee. Many radicalised Zealots who escaped to Jerusalem ended up in a vicious civil war with the more moderate Jewish leadership inside Jerusalem, while the Romans besieged the city. Eventually the Romans broke through, and as one might expect, many people were slaughtered and the Temple was destroyed.

There were three points of reference for Judaism – the Torah (scriptures); the land, which meant they could live as an autonomous people and not be slaves; and the Temple. The Temple was revered as the focus of the presence of God among the people. It represented God's favour of his chosen people. It was the symbolic centre of Judaism just as Mecca is the symbolic centre of Islam. It also served as the supreme judicial and administrative authority. When it was destroyed, it was so much more than the destruction of a building – the symbolic heart of Judaism was torn from the body of the people.

The religious, administrative and judicial structure disappeared. Many people were scattered, were sold as slaves or were sent to the mines. The regrouping of the Jewish people was going to be very difficult. Judaism needed to re-establish its identity. What did it mean to be Jewish in a world where there was no Temple, the anchor which held everything in place? What did it mean to be Jewish when they had been forced from the Promised Land into slavery, hard labour or forced emigration? One of the first things to suffer was tolerance of the various sects within Judaism itself. There was no longer the land, nor the Temple. The only emblems of identity were the scriptures and the Law. Very clear lines had to be drawn between those who believed both in the Jewish scriptures and the Jewish law, and those who believed any way differently. This was when the Jesus movement became something more distinct and separate from

Judaism and began to forge its own identity. The followers of Jesus were not one distinct homogenous group. There were variations in ethnicity and culture. What we now call 'gospels' grew out of the various groups creating their own sense of identity, their sense of belonging. Another factor in the creation of the gospels was the death of the generation of followers who knew Jesus, who followed him in life and witnessed to his message after his resurrection. There was a need to gather up this information in a form that could be kept safe.

Gospels are not biographies of Jesus. Neither are they journalism, the first-century equivalent of *The Tablet* or the *National Catholic Reporter*, reporting live on events. The gospels were written long after Jesus' own lifetime, for quite specific communities. The needs and concerns of the community were very much in the mind of the writer in the telling of the story. The Gospel of Mark was quite likely to have been written for a Christian community who lived in Syria which was at this time a Roman province. Mark very much focuses on the theology of the cross – everything must be interpreted through the reality of the cross. It is generally accepted that Mark's was the first gospel to be written. Matthew and Luke make use of Mark along with a collection of Jesus's sayings, gathered up by a different independent source.

The Gospel of Matthew was probably written for a Jewish Christian community in Antioch. The process of Judaism attempting to redefine itself would have been quite significant for this group. These Jewish Christians would have found themselves alienated from the larger Jewish community to which they had belonged, socially, culturally and ethnically. This must have been quite a painful experience, particularly in a society that valued the wider clan and tribal connections. It is also likely that there were significant tensions within this Jewish Christian group. There would have been blood links and marriage links with the Jewish community. Links such as these are not broken without significant upset and pain. This gospel was written out of a sense of displacement and alienation.

Luke was a well-educated second-generation (possibly third-generation) Christian. His gospel is the most polished in style and story. It is accepted that he is also the author of the Acts of the Apostles, which together with the Gospel of Luke form one book. Luke's focus is on salvation – Jesus is the fulfilment of God's promise. He does not single out any one event, such as the Crucifixion. For Luke the whole life of Jesus is significant. Significant in the faith it inspires and the challenge it offers to those who want to follow him. Hence the infancy stories which Luke included in his gospel. He needed to show that Jesus was marked out as special or chosen from the very beginning. This would be in keeping with the kind of storytelling of any hero across many cultures. Their birth and/or early childhood is shown to be auspicious in some way.

The gospels of Mark, Matthew and Luke are very similar and are called synoptic gospels. This means they can be viewed side by side for similarities and differences. The Gospel of John is very different. He focuses on light and darkness, on life and death. He is continually mining the deeper meaning of Jesus' words. John's gospel tends to be favoured by those who see themselves as 'spiritual'. John's community were Christian Jews. Again, as with some of the other early Christian communities, conflict, both within the group and with the wider Jewish community, influences the writing. John speaks of the 'Jews' in quite a scathing way, but they are not the Jews who were contemporaries of Jesus, rather they are the leaders of the Jews after the Roman defeat. These leaders, because they were struggling to gather their people and redefine themselves, were strongly opposed to the new Christian movement within its ranks.

The gospels are stories. They have plots and characters. They involve conflict, tension and the resolution of conflict. Each of the evangelists has an agenda – a purpose. Even though the central story is essentially the same, the emphases differ widely. They tell the story of Jesus. They draw out the consequences for the particular community of followers of what it means to follow Jesus. This was no small thing. These communities claimed for Jesus that he was the

Messiah, the fulfilment of the Jewish hope in God. To put this in context, it needs to be understood that the Messiah was expected to be a military leader who would lead the Israelites to victory against the oppressor (and there were many oppressors throughout the history of the Jews), who would restore the state to a place of power and glory. The Jesus of the gospels was a radically different person. It is difficult to imagine anybody more unlike the Messiah of the Hebrew scriptures.

The gospels are just one part of what we call the scriptures. The scriptures are a collection of writings from the Hebrew tradition as well as the new Christian tradition. It must not be forgotten that Jesus was a Jew – he was born a Jew and he died a Jew. What Christians call the Old Testament were the scriptures of his religious practice and were also the scriptures of the early Christian communities. Judaism did not become irrelevant with the rise of Christianity and many of its ideas, attitudes, practices and beliefs infused Christianity. It was over time, as writings started to circulate among the communities, and the deaths occurred of the companions and early disciples of Jesus, that the idea of a 'new' testament evolved.

What we now call the Christian bible was only formed in the last years of the fourth century CE. It is not one book, but a library of books. It contains, among others, history, prophecy, poetry, stories, and books of law. Some are very long books, some quite short. The scriptures, as gathered, represent the constant striving of men and women to understand what God is and what God wants of us. To speak of it as the word of God, is not to claim literal truth for every syllable in it. It is the work of human beings, inspired by the Holy Spirit certainly, but always writing as human beings. To start taking the bible literally does violence to it. It is a living word, not a dead script preserved in amber. It represents a long tradition of our encounter with God, initially as an oral tradition and then as a written tradition. It is open to speaking to each new generation who meets it in its own life setting. This is reflected in the type of writing that occurs in the bible. Those that were first written in Greek show influences of Greek philosophy and culture. Writing styles of the various books reflect the literary styles and conventions of the time they were written. The epic narratives, styles and form of poetry used were similar to other semitic societies in the Middle East. The wisdom traditions of Israel reflected those of other contemporary cultures also. There are very interesting similarities between the story of the flood in the Mesopotamian epic Gilgamesh and the story of Noah's ark in the bible.

One very simple example of the danger of a literal reading is the well-known story of the destruction of Sodom and Gomorrah (Gen 19:1–29). This is frequently used as a condemnation of homo-sexuality. However, a closer reading shows that it is a condemnation of the lack of hospitality to strangers. In ancient times to be a traveller on the road at night was to be at risk of attack by thieves and murderers. Hospitality to the stranger was built into the Hebrew code of behaviour because of their own experience of exile and desert wanderings. When Lot refuses to let the townsmen attack and rape his guests, he offers his two daughters to them instead: 'Look, I have two daughters, who have not known a man; let me bring them out to you, and do to them as you please; only do nothing to these men, for they have come under the shelter of my roof' (Gen 19:8). To read this literally is to accept the abuse and rape of two young women (probably in their early teens as they were not yet married) as reasonable and God-sanctioned and infinitely preferable to male rape. This is just one example, there are others.

The bible is really about the sense of God's participation in the completeness of people's lives as they live in the world with all its complications. Real flesh-and-blood life has its share of struggles and hardships, crises and resolutions, wars and peace, joys and sorrows, loves and hates. God's journey with his people is to be found in the middle of all this, not somewhere above and beyond, remote from it. The bible is the record of this engagement. It grew from the community, piecemeal over many centuries, through many writers. It is not a museum piece to be accorded respect but kept safely in the hands of custodians. It is the well from which we draw the living water.

CHAPTER TWO

Church: A Building or a People?

During some of the discussions on the desire for church reform and renewal that have happened in recent years, the phrase 'we are the Church' has arisen. Some clerics have dismissed this phrase, perhaps in fear of what the democratic overtones of what we truly means. Maybe they do not realise that it was a phrase used by Pope Pius XII in 1946 to remind newly appointed cardinals of active participation of all the faithful in building the community of church. Happily, others have embraced the term. But this is no little spat about the use of words. How we define ourselves will define how we behave, towards each other and to those who we perceive as 'outside' our group. This concept of church as the people is another link with Christianity's Jewish roots. The separation of church and state is a relatively recent phenomenon in history. The Jewish people would have made no distinction between politics and religion. God and the Law were what ruled their lives. Matters that might today be considered social, economic or political would all have been in-corporated in terms of God and the Law.

As previously mentioned, Israel's history has been quite turbulent – from slavery to independence to imperial domination, to exile, to being a client state. It was during one of the exiles that the concept of the regular gathering of the people became more formalised. When the Babylonians were the superpower in the Middle East (587 BCE), they invaded Palestine and destroyed the Temple and almost all its fortified towns. They captured the ruling classes and the skilled craftsmen from among the Jewish people and deported them to Babylon. The reason these were deported is because they were the leaders and opinion-formers. These would have been selected to avoid the possibility of rebellion.

The poor were left to work the land. The poverty and misery afflicting those left behind can only be imagined. The ruling classes mentioned above also included the religious leadership. So a significant segment of the educated Jewish people found themselves transplanted to a strange land for a period lasting almost forty years. With their usual pragmatic attitude they settled in and tried to function as best they could without losing their particular identity. This was helped by the fact that Judaism was more than a religion – it was a way of life. It was the identity of the people *as a people* rather than the identification of the people with a nation state. It also helped that they were allowed build houses and earn their living in any way they could. It is possible that they were not scattered throughout the land but kept in the same area so that they could be watched more easily. Essentially, there was a Jewish enclave in Babylon that was allowed to go about its business without much interference.

During this exile, two things developed great importance for the Jews: tradition and the Law. Both of these helped to distinguish them from the surrounding culture. It was at this time, in the absence of the Temple, that synagogue worship developed. The written word, the only portable means of expression of self-identity became central as it was collected and expanded. The word synagogue comes from the Greek. It is derived from the word *synago*, which means to bring people together. But its meaning is more than just bringing people together – it is about gathering people to achieve a meeting of minds. The meaning is very similar to another Greek word, *ekklesia*, also derived from a word meaning 'to call together' which was used by Greek-speaking Jews. So initially the term synagogue meant the group of people gathered together, not a building.

The concept of synagogue did not disappear when the Jewish people returned to Palestine after the Babylonians were, in their turn, defeated by the Persian empire. Though the priority of the former exiles was to reconstruct the Temple, they brought the idea of synagogue home with them. However, it was not until the second century BCE, that the synagogue began to occupy a place of greater importance in Jewish life. At this time it was still a term for the gathering of people. People met in private homes, or, if numbers dictated, in public rooms. With the destruction of Jerusalem after the rebellion against the Romans in 66–70 CE, the synagogue began its evolution into the organisation that was responsible for the preservation and fostering of Jewish life. It increasingly took on an institutional form, developing leadership roles and setting down prescribed methods of instruction. It was only later, in the second and third centuries CE, that a distinct architectural form for an identifiable building began to develop, and the name synagogue was applied to the building.

Likewise, in the fledging Christian communities, the term *ekklesia* was also used. Similar to *synago*, *ekklesia* also meant an assembly of people called together. This was for either political or entertainment purposes. The Greek-speaking Jews used this term for the gathering of the faith community for worship, information or instruction. It is not surprising then, that the earliest Christians adopted this term, *ekklesia*, for their gatherings.

There is direct evidence from scripture that the early Christian assemblies took place in private houses. Before very long, people were differentiating between the wealthier members and the less well-off, so some rules were laid down about how the individual assemblies were to be conducted. It is the collection of these individual assemblies throughout certain districts or areas that began to be called 'churches' – the church of the Thessalonians, the church at Corinth, the churches at Galatia. Implicit in this name of 'church' was not only the specific community at a particular location, but also the wider community of believing Christians throughout the Roman-dominated world at the time. So church described the community of the faithful rather than a structured, hierarchical model of church. The church developed through the human striving

27

to interpret the experience of Jesus in their lives. When we hear the oft-quoted piece of scripture, 'You are Peter, and on this rock I will build my church', it is well to remember that the whole top-down structure that has developed over time is hardly what Jesus had in mind – especially when one looks at the totality of the gospels and the lessons he left us by how he lived his own life.

In any group or gathering there needs to be some kind of leadership structure. It is important to understand that such structures are built on the existing cultural experience. The dominant culture in the early church was both Greek and Roman civilisation and this was the overwhelming influence on it. Greek philosophy, especially, played a highly influential role in the thinking of the early church leaders. No small part of that influence was the division between the physical and the spiritual – commonly referred to as dualism. This has been quite destructive historically because life was seen as a striving from the physical to the spiritual, with the body being regarded as simply the temporary vessel for the soul. This resulted in quite a negative view of the body gaining the upper hand. This negativity brings much in its wake in terms of the value of our bodies as worthy of respect in and of themselves and as sexual beings. So the development of the church reflected the surrounding culture – it did not, and does not, exist outside time, space and culture.

Given the highly stratified structure church has become, it may surprise many to know that there was no 'laity' in the early church. There was no such concept in the church of the first century. The word laity existed prior to the Christian era, and referred to the people of a locality as opposed to the ruling administration. The words used to describe the people in the New Testament derive from the Greek word *kleros*. This was the object used to draw lots. It could be pieces of bone, pebbles, bits wood, or potsherds – anything on which the name or mark of the person could be inscribed. The *kleroi* were put into a pot, shaken about and whoever's name was drawn out was selected for whatever the lot was drawn. In the New

Testament the words derived from *kleros* implied inheritance, share, lot, chosen, set apart. The new communities of faith saw themselves as being 'elected' or set apart, not as a special group above anyone else, but in the sense of the new life in Christ. There was no distinct priesthood, as we understand it today. There was no distinct priesthood as understood in Jewish terms either. There was a sense of the priesthood of all the people, which is beautifully articulated in the first letter of Peter: 'But you are a chosen race, a royal priesthood, a holy nation, God's own people, in order that you may proclaim the mighty acts of him who called you out of darkness into his marvellous light.' (1 Pet 2:9). The wider sense of the community of Christians took precedence over particular functions. The church was not clerical, nor was it lay. These terms did not apply – it was simply the church of the faithful: all the people were 'chosen'. The unity of the Christian community took precedence over the diversity of the various roles.

There was a reference to 'laity' in church for the first time towards the end of the first century – but it had a very brief appearance in a letter by an early bishop of Rome. It was towards the end of the second century of the Christian era that the term 'laity' appears again, but this time with a bit more presence. When, by the end of the second century, the term gains more traction, it enters the church vocabulary in a more definite way. However, that entry is not as hopeful as it might first appear. The 'laity' was not representative of the community at large. Rather it was a smaller, more elite group that evolved as the distinct class of clergy was evolving. The lay person was male, only married once and could baptise and make an offering in the absence of clergy. Among the laymen there were those who provided important functions in the community, one of the most important, and highly regarded was that of teaching. The lay man also fulfilled the roles of catechist and lector. As a catechist, his role was to instruct catechumens (those preparing for baptism). He did not involve himself in the more advanced teaching required for the educated Christian anxious to improve his or her theological knowledge. The lector not only read scripture for the community, but also interpreted it for those present. Over time, the layman's role began to be taken over by the members of the clergy, until, by the end of the third century, it had more or less disappeared. The roles of teacher and catechist were completely taken over, the role of the lector was reduced from reader/interpreter to just reader.

Women could not achieve the status of 'layperson', simply by virtue of being female. However, widows and virgins had a special status, with widows having a special role of prayer for the community. But even within that, there was a distinction. In a document called the *Apostolic Tradition*, a document from the third century, it makes clear that only a widow whose husband are dead a long time should be 'instituted' to the order of widows that were given a special place in the community. However, 'if her husband has been dead for only a short time, she should not be trusted.' Baptised women surely played an important part in the development of Christianity. Wealthy baptised women were certainly influential in the growth of Christianity as it spread throughout the Roman empire. Even if their husbands were immune to their attempts at evangelisation, their children were not.

It took until the fourth century before women were acknowledged as laypeople in the church. By then the clerical caste had already evolved, become more distinct and had assumed most, if not all, of the varied roles within the Christian community. This exclusion of women is hardly surprising when one considers how women were treated in the wider community. The cultural assumptions about women and their role in society became embedded in the cultural assumptions of the emerging church. While they were often missing from the early texts, when mention was made of them, women were mostly denigrated as being morally and intellectually inferior. Women were assumed to be naturally subordinated to men. Women were viewed as either dangerous temptresses or paragons of virtue. A telling illustration is in an archaeological site in the hills above the ruins of ancient Ephesus, discovered in 1906. There are the remains of two sixth-century images of St Paul and his companion St Thecla. The two images are the same height, which is important in the language of iconography, as it means they are of equal importance. Each of the figures has the right hand raised in teaching gesture, which implies equal authority. While the image of St Paul is untouched with his eyes and upraised hand visible, somebody had scraped away the eyes and the hand of St Thecla. That one figure was damaged while the other was left intact means the damage to St Thecla's image cannot be ascribed to iconoclasts, who disfigured holy images in order to destroy their power. The message is quite clear – the woman's apostolic authority was blinded and silenced.

It is also interesting to note that in all the resurrection stories, Mary Magdalene is the primary figure to first meet the resurrected Jesus, the first to be given the Good News of the New Way and the New Life – the apostle to the apostles. Yet she ends up portrayed as a prostitute. There is no scriptural basis for labelling her thus. Pope Gregory I in the sixth century blended the Gospel images of several women into one and then gave this fictitious person the name of Mary Magdalene. On examining the evidence, all that was said of Mary of Magdala in the Gospel of Mark was that Jesus had cast seven demons from her, just that and nothing else. This depiction of Mary was infused with the image of the woman taken in adultery in the Gospel of John. Then the repentant sinner (from Luke's gospel) who bathed Jesus' feet with her tears and dried them with her hair was the third woman incorporated into the image. Lastly, there was the image of Mary of Bethany, whom, along with Martha and Lazarus were friends of Jesus. In John's gospel, she is depicted as anointing Jesus' feet with expensive ointment and then wiping them with her hair. From this we end up with a whole tradition in religious art of Mary Magdalene as the repentant prostitute.

By the fifth century, there were three distinct groups – clergy, monks and laypeople, with the clergy, headed by the bishops, securely in charge. Many bishops took on the trappings of princes.

St John Chrysostom, an early bishop, describes, disapprovingly it must be said, the status of many bishops thus:

> Prefects and city magistrates do not enjoy such honour as the magistrate of the church; for if he enters the palace, who ranks the highest, or among the matrons, or among the house of the great. No one is honoured before him.

It took a mere one hundred and fifty years, once it became a tolerated religion, for the Christian leadership to fall prey to the desire for power and esteem. Though there were voices within the episcopal ranks who challenged the princely aspirations, history has shown us that the trappings of power seduce very easily.

CHAPTER THREE

Tradition: As it was in the beginning, is now and ever shall be …

The word 'tradition' comes from the Latin word *tradere*, which means 'to hand down'. However, it is not strictly limited to that meaning alone. It can mean, among other things, to bequeath or to entrust. Thinking of a tradition as a bequest or something entrusted to one has a more dynamic meaning than simply handing down. Perhaps this dynamic interpretation can serve more usefully to explain the church's tradition. Tradition is the transmission of beliefs, doctrines and rites of celebration through the generations of the faithful. Therefore, how we understand church will influence how we see and understand tradition. Ecclesiology (from *ekklesia*, meaning 'assembly', and *logia*, meaning 'study of, or discourse about, something') is the word used to describe the nature, mission and structure of the church – what it is, what it does, how it does it. If an ecclesiology is top down with strong emphasis on hierarchy and strict division of roles, it will interpret tradition one way. If an ecclesiology is more egalitarian, more inclusive, it will interpret tradition in another way.

As stated in Chapter One, neither Jesus nor the twelve, nor the wider group of disciples wrote anything down. The message of the Good News was transmitted, as Yves Congar describes it, 'by words and actions, preaching and example, by the exercise of authority and by organisation'. It is not merely a static process of handing something on unchanged. It is an active and dynamic transmission of reflection, through which spiritual and theological insights are assessed, valued and passed on to the next generation. Tradition can be described as the 'living faith of the dead, not the dead faith of the living'. Another useful image of tradition is the woodcutter speaking of his great-grandfather's axe – the head has been replaced once, and the handle replaced twice by the time he inherited it. Yet, for him, it is still his great-grandfather's axe, because it represents more than the actual tool that is the axe. It carries part of the family history and experience that connects the generations in a non-tangible way, yet it is very real.

Sometimes, the impression is given that the tradition of the church has been handed down intact from the apostles through an unbroken line and has not been interfered with in any way. Like much of what we know about church, it is more complicated than that. Given that much Catholic theology is based on the concept of tradition having divine authority, tradition needs some unpicking to understand it.

It is through tradition that a community consolidates its identity. The community can be a national community, a faith community, a tribal community, a sporting organisation, etc. Patterns of behaviour are established to allow the community to bond, to function and to expand as it develops. The identity begins to be formed through common aspirations and goals, agreed laws, through shared symbols and ceremonial rites. Tradition may be neatly summed up as community, creed, code and cult (the word cult is used here in the broad sense of ceremonies and rites). As it grew from a small community into an ever-larger group, Christianity needed to define itself. It developed in different cultural settings around the Mediterranean, and found ways to locate itself within these different cultural settings. There was also the need for Christianity to define itself within its own ranks. Because the fledgling church was still in flux, it was inevitable that disputes would arise. Remember, there was no handbook supplied by Jesus for this thing called 'church'. The canon of scripture had not yet been defined. It became evident that the expected return of the risen Christ was not going to happen any time soon, so the community needed to 'dig in' as it were. By the second century, the early Christians had to start the process of agreement on the sources of authentic teaching. As can be imagined this was neither easy, nor straightforward, but they began to define what it was to be a Christian.

Over time those who disputed the received ideas of church were called heretics. This word, as it has become to be understood, is quite negative. The implication is that heretics were out to cause trouble, trying to damage the church. As it happens, 'heretics' were often motivated by very strong feelings about their understanding of church, and believed that they were doing the right thing. I remember, as a child, being told about Martin Luther and the Reformation. He was presented as a 'heretic' (a word spoken with great disdain) whose sole purpose was to damage the church and 'do the devil's work'. Several decades passed before I learned that Martin Luther was actually a Catholic priest – a member of the Augustinian order. Luther was so horrified about the abuses within the hierarchy of the church at large that he wanted to bring about change and reform. There were several opportunities where the reforms he looked for could have been achieved, thus averting any schism. But the opportunities were squandered and we have been left with the scandal of a divided Christianity. So the word heretic needs to be used carefully, with a bit more humility by those who constantly see the world as sharply divided between 'them and us'.

The tradition of the church came to be understood and defined not just through the insights gained through prayer, the study of philosophy and the study of sacred writings, but also through challenging those people who subsequently were labelled as heretics. By the sixteenth century, prior to the Reformation, there were three main strands of thought about tradition. One strand held that the scriptures, explicitly or implicitly, contained all the truth needed for salvation. Tradition was needed for the correct interpretation of scripture, especially for what was implicit in the texts. The second strand held that revelation (the self-communication of

God through the life, death and resurrection of Jesus Christ) was contained partly in the scriptures and partly in the traditions believed to be passed down from the apostles through their disciples. The third strand held that scripture, apostolic traditions *and* the teachings of popes and of church councils were all authoritative and binding on the faithful. This was held to be so by the belief that the Holy Spirit remains with the church, inspiring and guiding it.

At the Council of Trent held after the Protestant Reformation, all three strands had their advocates. Eventually the Council agreed that the scriptures alone were not sufficient as a source of doctrine, that tradition played a vital role. When the draft document was prepared on this, it stated that revelation was partly in the written books and partly in the unwritten tradition. However, when the final texts were written, the 'partly ... partly' had been dropped, which left the question open. Trent held that that tradition, being divinely inspired, had an authority that was not less than scripture, and asserted that they both be received with equal respect and reverence. The Council of Trent sat for three periods between 1545 and 1563 (there was a gap of three years between first and second period, and ten years between second and third). It brought about many badly needed reforms. The church was in an appalling state by the beginning of the sixteenth century, with popes and many bishops taking on all the trappings of secular monarchy with great enthusiasm. The diocesan clergy were very poorly trained and not equipped to lead parishes.

Much of great value was achieved at Trent. There is a great wisdom in stating a general principle for something, and by doing so, leaving the question open. Trent managed this by stating that traditions that should be binding on the faithful be restricted to faith and morals rather than including traditions that arose through custom and discipline. Unfortunately, there are those who cannot cope with the idea of the open question, and need to pin everything down to its last detail. This results in an excessively legal interpretation on matters of faith, usually spoken of as a 'juridical interpretation'. This is what happened in the years after Trent, until we ended up with a stifling, rule-bound Catholicism that existed prior to Vatican II. It owed more to canon law than to the inspiration of scripture.

Given that the Council of Trent resulted largely from the schism of the Reformation, it became a definition of Catholicism over and against Protestantism, rather than something organic within Catholicism itself that allowed for development. In the decades and centuries following the Council, this hardening of Catholicism versus Protestantism became entrenched with much vitriol on both sides, none of it honouring the message of Jesus Christ. A simple example is the development of scripture studies within Protestantism in the early twentieth century. This was a fruitful field of study. The tools of literary and historical criticism were applied to scripture and many important insights resulted, which included the understanding that scripture ought not be taken as literal. Catholic scholars were forbidden to engage in this critical appreciation of scripture. So they lagged behind other Christian denominations in the new understanding of the text. Eventually in 1943 Pius XII allowed Catholics to take up biblical studies. Though they started almost fifty years behind their fellow-Christians, Catholic biblical studies flourished in the latter half of twentieth century. Through biblical scholarship it became obvious that there were diverse traditions within scripture, and studies in sociology highlighted the role of traditions in shaping and maintaining diverse cultures and societies.

As mentioned earlier, tradition as understood within Christianity is not just a question of 'handing on'. A helpful discernment on what tradition means came about as a result of ecumenical work being done within Protestantism during the 1920s and 1930s. There were two groups: one believing that doctrine divides, but that action unites; and another group believing that doctrinal agreement was critical to unity among Christians. After World War II, the issue was taken up again. Eventually, in 1963 the concept of tradition within faith communities was presented in a very useful and pragmatic way:

a) Tradition – with a capital 'T' – is the process of handing on the tradition, the process of transmission.

b) tradition – with a lower case 't' – is the content of what is being transmitted.

c) traditions – lower case 't' and plural – the particular, distinctive modes of understanding and celebrations of the local churches that are inherited and culturally conditioned.

It should have become obvious by now that tradition does not exist outside and apart from culture. It is inextricably linked. Tradition has a value in that it distils the experience and wisdom of those who have gone before. Succeeding generations can build on this experience, knowledge, wisdom and skill, and so develop and evolve. Simply put, tradition saves us from having to reinvent the wheel in each new generation.

Tradition helps form us as human beings, but we in turn, as human beings, mould tradition. Where tradition is dynamic, holding the past and present in a creative tension, it fosters growth to maturity. It enables adults to take responsibility for themselves and the wider community. It promotes the group identity and continuity, yet remains open to the possibility of development and change. Where tradition is static and becomes an ideology, it limits freedom by the demand to conform. It stunts personal growth, restricting people to a kind of infantilism, waiting for the 'authority' to tell them what to do. Where tradition becomes an ideology, there is an almost inevitable regression into a tribal attitude with its inherent prejudices. This regression into ideology was what happened in the Catholic Church during the course of the three hundred and fifty years after the Council of Trent. As the secular power of the church diminished, and the papal states were lost, its only expression of power was that which it exerted over its own members.

A problem arises with tradition where people through their education in the broader world see it as something that fences in and limits, thus hampering freedom. Unfortunately, if critical analysis is not brought to bear on tradition, everything that is good and life-giving about it can be cast off at the same time as that which is life-curtailing. Taking ownership of tradition as a free, mature adult needs critical engagement with it. A necessary part of this engagement with tradition is interpretation. Those who transmit and those who receive tradition need to relate it to their life situations and their experiences. They must interact with each other and interpret for each other their past and present experiences.

One of the most remarkable responses to tradition and its place is in the bible, and it is the story of Abram/Abraham and the attitude of the apostles, Jesus' own followers (For Abraham's full story see Gen 12:1–25:11). Abram was blessed by God, who made a covenant with him, guaranteeing him a great progeny. As a sign of this covenant, Abram's name was changed to Abraham – he was starting a new stage in his life and a new name was appropriate. The bible story of Noah speaks of God's covenant after the flood, promising never to send such a deluge again, and the sign of the covenant would be the rainbow – a one-sided covenant, as it were. With Abraham, God makes a covenant, but states that Abraham must also actively participate in the covenantal relationship. The sign of this covenant? Circumcision. Abraham was to be circumcised and also every male in his household and wider clan including slaves, whether born within the family or bought in: 'So shall my covenant be in your flesh an everlasting covenant.' From then on, every male child was to be circumcised also. Any uncircumcised male who refuses circumcision is to be cut off from his people because he is seen as breaking the covenant. Circumcision was nothing less than the outward sign of the covenant made by God with his people. The importance of this cannot be over-estimated. So circumcision became an immensely important tradition among the Jewish people. A refusal to submit to circumcision was nothing less than the breaking of the covenant with God.

When the first members of the Christian assembly began their preaching about Jesus Christ and moving outward into the non-Jewish, Gentile lands, naturally the issue of circumcision arose. It was, after all, the mark of the covenant with God. There were those who insisted that circumcision was necessary. Given the long tradition and its meaning within Judaism, such a stance was not surprising. After some debate on the issue in Antioch, Paul and Barnabas went to Jerusalem to the apostles and elders to get a ruling (usually called the Council of Jerusalem). After much debate and discussion Peter addressed the group saying that God knows the human heart and makes no distinctions. Then James, who seems to have been the leader of the Jerusalem Christians, made a ruling: so long as the Gentiles were turning to God, they should not be obliged to be circumcised. The Law still applied to the Jewish members of the assembly, but not to the Gentiles. A tradition probably some three thousand years standing could be mitigated, if the Good News of God's incarnation in Jesus Christ was to be hindered.

Tradition is not just about the past, it is also about the present and how we proceed into the future – it is a living thing. A useful metaphor was used in *Dei Verbum*, the document on revelation from Vatican II:

> This sacred Tradition, then, and the sacred Scripture of both Testaments, are like a mirror, in which the Church, during its pilgrim journey here on earth, contemplates God, from whom she receives everything, until such time as she is brought to see him face to face as he really is.
>
> *Dei Verbum*, n. 7 (See Flannery)

The mindset that gave us this insight was light years away from Pius IX when at the First Vatican Council in 1870, he declared without shame or embarrassment: 'I am the tradition.' This outburst was as a result of contribution by a bishop explaining at the Council that the pope, when teaching, is assisted by the advice of the bishops who embody the tradition of the churches. This was to make clear that a pope does not teach as an isolated monarch, but as first among the bishops. Pius IX sent for the bishop and castigated him, accusing him of treachery. The hapless bishop replied that he had only said that bishops are witnesses to the tradition. The pope reacted with incredulity: 'Witnesses to the tradition? *I* am the tradition!'

If understood as living and dynamic, tradition includes both continuity and change. When we look at scripture, we see that Jesus was in continuity with the Law and prophets of the Jewish scriptures. Yet he reinterpreted the tradition to create a new way of looking at the world. his view minimised the importance of rituals, and placed significant importance on personal responsibility and the place of justice in dealing with others. As a transmitter of the reinterpreted tradition, he was changed himself. He went from an unknown Galilean, living and working in a small rural village to being someone that was perceived as a threat to the governors of Palestine, and so was executed. The receivers of the tradition interpreted by him were also changed because they left their old lives to follow him. The tradition itself was changed and moved from a Jewish sect into a broad movement with an impetus and momentum of its own.

Tradition is more than the sum of its parts. It is more than doctrines, than teachings, than encyclicals and other formal pro-nouncements, though it contains them. The relationship of scripture and tradition is an ongoing discussion in church. Ronald Witherup in his book on *Dei Verbum* sums it up perfectly: 'Tradition embraces the living practices of the community of faith, as well as the biblical history that led to the birth of the church.'

CHAPTER FOUR

Doctrine and Dogma

Doctrine and dogma refer to the teachings of the Catholic Church. Historically, the principal teaching authority of the church was the local bishop. Bishops were the leaders of the Christian community and it was their responsibility to see that the community functioned properly. Over time, as the church grew and various disputes arose, bishops from the same territory would gather together to discuss the problem. Such a gathering would be convened especially if the issue threatened the unity of the community. These gatherings became known as synods. The word 'synod' comes from the Greek (via Latin) and roughly translates as 'same way' (with 'way' having the sense of travel). So, synods were about finding a way through the problem or dispute so that all could agree on a solution and go forward together. This sounds very agreeable, but sometimes synods could be quite fractious affairs, with tempers running very high. As the church became ever more widespread throughout Europe and the Near East, issues of significance for the universal church arose that went to the heart of the faith. These events required larger synods, with more participants, which became known as councils (see Chapter Five).

Developing from the tradition of leadership in the local community, the world's bishops, as a group, eventually understood their role as the teaching authority of the church. This includes the pope, whose primary title is actually Bishop of Rome. This teaching authority of the bishops is known as the *magisterium*. This is a Latin word for the role or office of superintendant, president or master.

From this we get verbs that speak of control, governance and instruction or teaching. *Magisterium* was a word used by the ancient Romans in the secular world in the context of political governance (The English word magistrate comes from *magister*). In mediaeval times, there was the *magisterium* of the theologians, the authority that theologians had by virtue of their education. However, by the nineteenth century, this had disappeared and the term became restricted to the hierarchy. Increasingly, in the twentieth century, the term seems to have acquired an ever more restricted use, that of papal *magisterium*. This is quite limiting on the term and is a negative development when viewed in terms of church teaching. 'Teaching' presented as imposition or diktat is not true teaching.

Doctrine and dogma are two words that are often used interchangeably. However, they are two separate, but closely related, things. The distinction between them is important. Doctrine might be loosely described as how we reflect on what we believe, and then how we share that reflective faith with others. It is an expression of the *ekklesia's* insight into the meaning of the words and deeds of Christ. Dogma is a formal statement from the teaching authority of the church on some aspect of that doctrine that the faithful are obliged to believe.

Both dogma and doctrine are intimately related to revelation (God's self-disclosure in Jesus Christ). The whole church is entrusted with the word of God, that is, all the baptised members. The early church's proclamation that Jesus died for humanity; that he died and was buried and that he was raised to life on the third day in accordance with the scriptures; that Jesus was the Christ – the anointed one of God, is *the* basic doctrine of the Christian Church. This basic doctrine – the life, death and resurrection of Jesus – was reflection upon, studied, written about. From this there was the development of writings that eventually became the New Testament. These writings formed the early teachings of the church. As we saw in Chapter One, the gospels arose out of very specific life circumstances of the Christian communities. Therefore, there will be particular emphasis in the doctrine being explained in those writings. For example, the doctrine of the Gospel of Mark is that Jesus is the crucified Messiah; the doctrine of the Gospel of John is that Jesus is the eternal Word or Wisdom of God. The understanding of the word of God unfolds over time and in particular historical contexts. It is believed within church that this process of understanding is infused by the inspiration of the Holy Spirit. This does not mean that we always get it right, that we will not make mistakes, because we do. History is littered with the evidence – the treatment of Galileo is just one obvious example. But we believe that this care and guidance through and by the Spirit will eventually lead us to the truth.

The New Testament is the primary source of Christian doctrine, but not the only source. The meaning of Christ's life for the Christian community can be expressed in several ways – through preaching, in the liturgies (the Easter Triduum, for example), the works of theologians, in the lives of women and men who actively live out the gospel in their daily lives. So tradition also plays an important role in doctrine. Christian doctrine is also expressed in papal encyclicals and other various pronouncements. Though the various ways in which doctrine is expressed in and through church are many, scripture must *always* be its touchstone.

During various turbulent times in the early church (see Chapter Two), it became necessary to formally define what was understood to be authentic and true about the faith. These are the dogmatic statements. Early examples of such dogmatic statements set down what was to be believed regarding Christ's divinity and his humanity. There were also dogmatic statements made about the understanding of the Trinity and about Mary being the mother of God. Quite apart from the 'big' questions that end up being defined dogmatically, much doctrine is given voice in the various papal documents. These documents are meant to speak with authority, but not about matters dealing with revelation, or matters considered unchangeable. The papal encyclical (a word derived from Latin and

Greek, meaning circular, because the document was circulated among the faithful) is meant to perform an important teaching service within the church, along with bishops' pastoral letters. They are usually written to respond to particular concerns, happening at a particular time. For example, the encyclical *Rerum Novarum* (Of New Things) promulgated by Leo XIII in 1891. This document was a response to the issues arising from the shift from farming to working in industrial employment in the cities during the industrial revolution. Workers' conditions and the rights and dignity of labour were the concern of this encyclical. It was a landmark document in that it was the first of a series of such documents that continued to be written through the twentieth century on social justice.

The primary purpose of doctrine within the church is to allow each member of the faithful to internalise the meaning of what Christ is for the world, and to make it their own. The meaning is not meant to be a legal list of 'dos' and 'don'ts' but something that relates to people's lives in the actual, concrete situations in which they find themselves. The truths contained in the doctrines of the church are one thing, the manner and means of how these are expressed is a different thing. Sometimes the statement of doctrine ceases to be something fluid and dynamic and ends up being choked by legalistic formulations. Truths are eternal. The understanding and expression of truths in any given historical era is culturally conditioned. Understood in this way, doctrine is something alive and dynamic. They are meant to be signposts to the truth, not the actual truth itself.

The use of the word dogma has not remained the same through church history. It is only from c.1800 CE that in Catholic usage it has been given a precise meaning of: 'A divinely revealed truth which is proposed by the public judgement of the church as to be believed with divine faith, so that the contrary doctrine is condemned by the church as heretical' (St Philip Neri). Before this, the term was much looser and could mean a decree, decision, opinion or doctrine. A decree of Caesar, such as the census mentioned in Luke's gospel would have been an imperial dogma. Ancient philosophical schools would have had their own dogmata (plural of dogma) which were their defining tenets. This distinction of the use of the word dogma is important when looking at older church documents prior to St Philip Neri's definition above. Earlier use of the term would not have had the same emphasis on the definitive nature of the doctrine proposed by the teaching authority.

Can doctrine and dogma evolve and change? The simple answer is: yes, they can and do. They may change slowly, may not change in a straight line, but they do change. Also, it must be noted that not all changes are for the better. However, you would be hard-pressed to get a church leader to admit this reality of change publicly. This is due mainly to a hangover from the times when the church saw itself as the perfect society – the church is of God, God is perfect, ergo the church is perfect, and cannot err in matters of doctrine. The most that will usually be admitted is that the truth declared in a doctrine or dogma can be more fully understood and better explained at a different time because of the advance in the sciences, including social sciences and anthropology.

It is useful to look at a few areas where teaching has changed. Firstly, and most obviously, is the anti-Semitism that has been a part of the church for most of its history. It has its roots in scripture. This should be a warning about taking scripture out of context and taking it literally. One cannot read scripture without looking at the political issues of the time and what was involved in the separation of the early Christian Jews from the greater Jewish population.

Even though some popes certainly upheld the rights of Jews, official pronouncements on the Jews make it very clear how they were to be perceived by Christians. For example, in 1234 it was decreed in Arles, France that when outside their homes, all male Jews from age thirteen upwards were to wear a 'round badge of three or four fingers in width' and all women were to wear veils. If they did not comply, they were to be denied interaction with Christians. This was reinforced two hundred years later along with the decree that Jews be made live apart from Christians. This ethnic separation was again insisted upon by papal teaching in 1555, leading to what became known as the ghettos. Apart from formal decrees, letters from popes to bishops about how Jews should be treated also fuelled this anti-Semitism.

The softening of the anti-Semitic teachings in the Catholic Church began to be modified in the early part of the twentieth century, reaching a peak during the Second Vatican Council, when it decreed that the church 'deplores all hatreds, persecutions, displays of anti-Semitism levelled at any time or from any source against the Jews' (*Nostra Aetate*, n. 4. See Flannery). When an institution moves from wanting to brand and ghettoise the Jews to deploring all hatreds, persecutions and displays of anti-Semitism, it is nothing less than change. It is not just 'development'.

The same change is evident in the treatment of slaves and slavery in the doctrine of the church. Again, using St Paul as their guide, the church authorities endorsed slavery. Jesus' teaching that he was sent to preach the Good News to the poor, freedom to the captives and that the oppressed would receive justice, seemed to fade away into the background. There was a constant teaching justifying slavery, up to circa the seventeenth century. Even from then, despite some teaching that slavery was wrong, there was still ample teaching that it was acceptable. As late as the mid-nineteenth century, the Holy Office (now the Congregation for the Doctrine of the Faith (CDF)) taught that slavery was not contrary to natural and divine law. It is sobering to think that up to the mid-twentieth century segregation in churches was still a reality for black Catholics in the US where they suffered the same segregation in churches as they did every-where else.

This church teaching on slavery did not just 'develop' – it did an 180 degree turn! It moved from condoning it and the church leadership actually owning slaves, to becoming a champion of anti-slavery. It changed its teaching. Trying to claim that all change is, in fact, development is to insult the intelligence of the faithful. We recognise change when we see it. There is no shame in change. There is no shame it admitting we got it wrong. The damage is done pretending that change is not possible, that the change we can see is actually something else. This is the usual answer about change in church teaching. That it is not change, it is the same teaching but with better insights to draw out more fully what was already contained, hidden as it were, in the particular teaching.

Change is not only possible in church teaching, but is a reality when some teachings are just dropped – called by some 'reform by amnesia'. The teaching on Limbo was never a dogma of the church, that is, it was never formally defined. But it was a teaching of the church by tradition. However, by the 1940s seminarians in Ireland were being taught that it was a very shaky concept. By the Second Vatican Council in mid-1960s it was tacitly dropped. Limbo was also dropped from the 1992 revised Catechism of the Catholic Church. Bishop Allesandro Maggiolini of Como, who was on the original editorial team for the revised Catechism, had this to say:

> Certainly Limbo is not in the Catechism, but equally its existence is not denied either. It's wise not to insist too much on a kind of geography of the beyond, given that we are not capable of understanding its mysteries. It's best to shut up about what we don't know about.
>
> *National Catholic Reporter*, 28 May 1999

In 1985, Cardinal Ratzinger, in an extensive interview in Italian published in English as *The Ratzinger Report*, when asked about Limbo said, as part of his answer, 'Just let the concept of Limbo drop, if need be.' (A little editorial finesse influenced the English translation and modified this slightly to read: 'One should not hesitate to give up the idea of Limbo, if need be…') The tragedy is that all the parents of unbaptised babies who were stillborn or died shortly after birth cannot just dismiss the pain that resulted from the teaching about Limbo as easily.

To be human is to be fallible. The church is the Body of Christ but is created and peopled by flawed humanity and bears the stamp of that fallibility. The guidance and inspiration of the Holy Spirit remains with the church but can only be expressed through human beings who, through the exercise of their free will, can either honour that inspiration or impede it. In the development and framing of doctrine, the body of the faithful who comprise the greater part of the church have a role to play. John Henry Newman understood this. He has been quoted and misquoted many times, but I hope I am faithful to his thought here. He saw the laity as an essential resource for the teaching authority of the church. He called it the *consensus fidelium* (consent or agreement of the faithful) and saw it as a vital part of the church's tradition – as an indicator of the infallibility of the church as a whole. Newman had touched on something very important for the healthy growth of the church. But he paid dearly for his belief that the wider church membership had a vital role in discerning church teaching. His career in the church stalled. Newman was even accused of heresy by an English bishop. A secretary/confidant of Pius IX called him the 'most dangerous man in England!' Although it is worth mentioning, that same confidant, George Talbot, is described in Eamon Duffy's *Saints & Sinners* as being 'devious, feline, wreathed in intrigue, his view of the world and the church a perpetual game of cowboys and Indians, heroes and villains.'(p. 228). Newman's insight into the importance of consulting the lay membership was borne out more than a hundred years later. The teaching authority of the church ignored the *consensus fidelium* in the matter of its teaching on birth control and has paid a very high price indeed (see Chapter Nine).

Bernard Lonergan in his *Method in Theology* notes that 'individuals not only develop, but also suffer breakdowns, so too do societies'. Our church is a society of individuals in community, and it, too, is capable of breakdown. This is what we are seeing in Ireland, and in other countries, at the moment. But all is not lost. If we look to our 'originating value' which for us as Christians is the Jesus of Nazareth who is the Risen Christ, and apply what Lonergan calls

the transcendental precepts: be attentive, be intelligent, be reasonable, be responsible, then doctrine can be seen to be subject to change
without losing credibility. Nobody has had the last word on doctrine
and dogma yet, simply because this is not possible. Yet, integral to
our faith journey is the necessity to keep searching after the truth
and framing our insights in a language we can understand. The last
word cannot be uttered until the end of time when we find ourselves
living the reality for which we have hoped all our lives.

Chapter Five

The Papacy

The job of electing a pope falls to a small, select group within the church. Cardinals have had this role since the eleventh century, and the purpose of limiting the role to cardinals was to stop the interference of rulers and aristocracy in the choice of pope. Electing a pope was a political decision bound up with the secular politics of Europe. Sometimes the papacy was a pawn in the serious game of politics, and sometimes it was actively involved.

For all the discussion on the presence of the Holy Spirit in the choice of pope, plenty of back-room discussions take place. There are formal meetings, of course, but plenty of informal discussion takes place among various groups who hope to have 'their man' elected. This is no surprise, reading the history of popes is a lesson in political intrigue. Unfortunately, for the church, the role of pope as a global religious leader has for centuries been more a monarchical role than a truly religious leadership role. Many people may not realise it, but the pope's most important title is not that of pope, but as the Bishop of Rome. For it is as a bishop that the pope gains his authority of leadership.

Traditionally, the pope is seen as the successor of Peter, who is often mistakenly called the first pope. Peter was not a pope; even the earliest lists of popes that were compiled did not include him. There was no such thing as a pope in the early years of the church. The Christian communities elected their local leader. This person, in time, became known as a bishop, and fulfilled the role of elder in the community. A bishop had a pivotal role in deciding what was acceptable Christian teaching and what represented heresy. The care, unity and the flourishing of the community was his responsibility. A measure of a good bishop was that he was married with just one wife and well brought up children who respected their father's authority.

Just as there was not always a pope, neither was Rome always the centre of Christianity. The community at Jerusalem was seen as the most important in the very early church and that was lead by James, 'the brother of the Lord'. At different times, the churches at Antioch and Alexandria were also prominent in the Christian community and seen as having particular authority. Rome, as a place of authority, came somewhat later, although it was always accorded special respect. The Christian community in Rome were also Greek-speaking for the first 150 years or so, as it was an immigrant church at the beginning. Theologically, the church of the eastern part of the Roman empire was the most influential in the first few centuries. This was predominately Greek-speaking and most of the theological foundations of the church were laid here. The first ecumenical council of the church was in the eastern part of the Roman empire, at Nicaea. It was called together by the emperor Constantine, and the pope did not attend.

Tradition has it that both Peter and Paul were martyred in Rome. Therefore, the leader of the Christian community in Rome was accorded a particular respect. He was seen as succeeding to the leadership of Peter and Paul who died in defence of their faith. Given that Rome was the heart of the empire, there were also Christians of significant wealth here, who helped churches in other jurisdictions with financial aid. Also, in the great theological debates of the early church it suited the purposes of some to refer to Rome for support when they were not getting it elsewhere. The beginnings of a Roman ascendancy in the church began towards the end of the second century, when a Latin leader became Bishop of Rome. This bishop brought the discipline and vigour of the Roman way of doing things to his office.

The position of Rome as the centre of Christian leadership came into its own with the fall of the secular Roman empire. With the dismantling of the Roman political apparatus, it fell to those who ruled the religious structure to fill the vacuum. There was a ready-made template into which it could fit itself – therefore, much of the ecclesiastical structure is based on the Roman imperial model. Unfortunately, this set the church on the road to a monarchical, religious empire, with all the trappings of power that that entails. The Western Latin Church grew in power and importance in Europe and spread westwards. The Eastern Greek Church lost its dominance of Christianity, but remained a strong force. The Western and Eastern churches eventual split in the eleventh century. This is known as the Great Schism. This was the result of ongoing theological and political wrangling between Western and Eastern Christianity, in ways neither of which could be proud. With the split, each side excommunicated the other – a scandal that was only resolved at the time of Vatican II in the mid-twentieth century.

One of the problems of a monarchical papacy is the perception that popes had of themselves and of their role. Traditionally, for the first millennium the role was seen as being the Vicar of Peter (fulfilling the role of Peter). As the papacy become ever more powerful in the High Middle Ages, being the Vicar of Peter no longer satisfied. Other bishops could possibly claim apostolic origins for their territories also, therefore the primacy of the Roman See might be challenged. Pope Innocent III (1198–1216 CE) claimed the title Vicar of Christ for himself and subsequent popes. It was not enough to be considered a successor of the apostles, even one of the pre-eminent apostles, but the claim was no less than the Vicar of Christ. This is where we get the notion of the pope being 'God's representative on earth', from one man's exalted sense of his own prestige, status and dignity for the role he inhabited.

Reading a history of the popes is a very enlightening exercise. One can see how the individual personalities of the popes, and their sense of their own power and position, influenced the direction of the church – for good or for ill. It also helps to dismiss the notion that the pope is somehow 'God's representative on earth'. The pope is just a man, like any other, with the potential for the best and worst that is in any human being. Fostering the cult of the personality and exalting the incumbent does the papacy and the church no favour.

'Collegiality' is a term that has entered into the conversation about the pope and his place among the bishops of the church. This is not a newfangled concept coming from modern secular democracy. It comes from the Latin word *collegium*, meaning brotherhood, close association or colleagueship – all indicating an assembly as a group. The word and the concept existed since before the establishment of the church. The *collegium* in Roman law was an assembly or guild of people with the same mutual interests – anything from gatherings of business people, craftsmen or even thieves! Collegiality existed within the church itself, from the very beginning, in varying degrees, in reality, if not always in name. The 'college' of apostles led the beginnings of the early church, although they would not have used that term themselves. The 'college' of cardinals meeting together elects the pope. The 'college' of bishops is the worldwide group of bishops leading the local churches and form the leadership, together with the pope, of the universal church. It is from 'college' that we get the word 'collegiality', meaning to have joint responsibility in the sense of colleagues working together.

Unfortunately, for the development of the church, the definition of papal infallibility allowed some members of the hierarchy to inflate the role of the pope to absolute sovereign or ruler. Even though Pius IX was very much in favour of the definition of infallibility, and undermined those not in favour of it, it seems that he did not see his position as undermining the authority of the college of bishops. When the German bishops challenged a statement of Otto Von Bismarck (a devout Lutheran and the first Chancellor of a united Germany) Pius IX supported them. In a confidential communication to the German diplomatic corps Bismarck claimed that the pope's primacy within the Catholic

Church gave him jurisdictional rights over the bishops of any country. When this information became public, the German bishops reacted strongly. They made it clear that, although the pope is the leader of the church, he does not absorb the authority of other bishops. He is bishop of Rome, and Rome only, not the bishop of any other diocese. Pius IX issued two statements following the German bishops' statement, supporting and reaffirming their comments. Despite this, however, there were members of the church, at the time, who interpreted the role of the pope as absolute ruler, whose every utterance was infallible without distinction. This idea even went to the extremes for some who held that there was almost an incarnation of Christ in the pope. Even though such an opinion was confined to a small following, nevertheless, they were able to exert influence where it mattered.

What is called the centralisation of authority in the church began with the reforms of Pope Gregory VII in the eleventh century. The idea was not to deliberately establish a papal monarchy, but to attempt to reform a church that badly needed reform. It was also to disentangle the church from the political wrangling of various European monarchs and rulers. This papal monarchy continued right up until the First Vatican Council in 1870 and on through until the Second Vatican Council in 1962–5. This means that despite the comments of Pius IX about the pope not absorbing the authority of the local bishops, the papacy was, in effect, an absolute monarchy, with bishops in a more passive role. Jurisdiction of the pope over the universal church is one thing, the centralisation of power is a different matter altogether. Leadership is a necessary part of helping a group to function well, but leadership does not necessarily mean exercising absolute control.

By the time of the Second Vatican Council, the world had experienced the dismantling of political empires, the spread of democracy, two devastating wars, the revelations of the concentrations camps, a rise in the resistance to colonialism in Africa, and an increasingly educated population, not to mention the arrival of television, the consumer economy and the Cold War. Change was in the air. Change was just as important for the church as elsewhere.

One of the most important insights of the Second Vatican Council was the need to 'return to the sources'. This was an appreciation that the type of church that had grown from the Council of Trent in the sixteenth century and the First Vatican Council in the nineteenth century was not the only possible expression of the church. There was a wealth of experience to be mined in returning to scripture and the writings of the early Church Fathers, especially those who lived and flourished in the Eastern Church. At Vatican II, the gathered leaders understood that the idea of church needed to be redefined and understood in the light of the modern world.

The concept of collegiality among the bishops arose as part of the discussion on the church during Vatican II. There was a desire among the majority of bishops to work towards a conciliar definition of collegiality – how the authority of the bishops, together with the authority of the pope, was to work for the good of the universal church. There were differences in interpretation about what collegiality meant – some saw it from a very narrow legalistic viewpoint, others saw from a broader, most pastoral perspective. As with most of the Vatican II reforms, there was a small, but very vocal and determined group who set its face against any change. It did this in all of the debates in varying degrees of intensity and passion. This was evident also in the debates on collegiality. It must be stated here that collegiality was not an attempt to diminish the role of the pope, but rather to recover the proper ecclesial role of the bishops in the governance and leadership of the local churches, as part of the universal church.

In its recovery of the role of bishops, Vatican II gave a sacramental character to the college of bishops. It was not to be understood in legal terms, but as sacrament, through ordination. Collegiality was to be understood in terms of church as a pilgrim people, rather than as any legal right or privilege. When the vote was taken at the

Council on the propositions on collegiality, the votes were over-whelmingly in favour. Unfortunately, like so much else that grew from Vatican II, the concept of collegiality is honoured more in name than in actuality. One writer describes it as being 'grudgingly tolerated'. However, collegiality was not even 'grudgingly tolerated' during the papacy of John Paul II and Benedict XVI. Occasional lip-service was paid to it, certainly, but it was effectively ignored. Part of the 'problem' with collegiality is the perception that it is a threat to papal authority. This seems to be of particular concern to the Roman Curia. It does not take a giant leap of imagination to understand that the more the college of bishops own their authority, the lesser role there is in the universal church for the Roman Curia as a ruling body. There seems to have developed an idea that the Curia is somehow an intermediary between the pope and the college of bishops. This strange interpretation of the role becomes evident at synods of bishops.

Episcopal synods are meant to be an expression of collegiality as defined at Vatican II. These are meetings of bishops from particular territorial regions who gather to discuss issues specifically relevant to them. Or they can also be meetings on a particular subject, which will gather bishops from all over the world, e.g. the Synod on the Laity. However, these gatherings are tightly controlled by the Roman Curia. Bishops are sometimes told what they can or cannot say. In his book *Reform of the Papacy* Archbishop John Quinn cites the example of the Asian Synod in early 1998. The report on the speeches at this synod was written on Friday, 24 April, even though all the speeches had not been completed until Tuesday, 28 April, almost a full week later! Quinn makes the point in his book that holding all the synods in Rome allows too much curial influence and weakens the doctrine that the particular churches, together, constitute the universal church. This dilution of collegiality reduces bishops to the status of regional managers of a transnational corporation, with the chief executive officer and management team based at its head-quarters.

Mature adults take responsibility for themselves and their behaviour. Collegiality is important in allowing that maturity space to function. Creating a structure that mimics nature with an alpha male surrounded by subordinate males interferes with that mature responsibility. To speak of the papacy and episcopal hierarchical structure as being divinely ordained is questionable, particularly if one is familiar with Jesus' words in the New Testament. That is not to say that leadership is not important or necessary. Of course it is. No organisation can function properly without leadership. The more consultative and collegial that leadership is, the more positively it is likely to function. This is true of small organisations and large. But leadership is not a licence for domination, and certainly not in church. Not only should the leadership lead by example for its own members, but it ought to be an exemplar for the world as to how leadership should be exercised.

Much is made in Catholic teaching of the tradition that the pope and the bishops are the successors of Peter and the apostles. Again and again, one reads that the hierarchical structure is divinely ordained, and therefore cannot be otherwise. This influences the reading of scripture as the *dramatis personae* are already recognised and identified with. An interesting reading of scripture is to dispense with these preconceived identifications, and examine the behaviour of the various groups as they are described. Then compare the behaviour of the religious authorities of our time with the religious authorities of Jesus' time and see if similarities exist. It is an instructive exercise. Jesus was an ordinary Jewish man who had no ties to the religious elite. He was not a priest nor did he belong to the tribe from which the priests came. Yet he had no difficulty challenging the ruling religious authorities. He spoke against the outward marks and trappings of status and made clear that actions speak louder than words. Jesus made very clear that leadership through humble service was what was required by those who followed him, and that laws were for the benefit of humanity, humanity was not at the service of laws.

CHAPTER SIX

Councils: Twenty-One and Counting

In the context of church a general council is a large gathering of bishops from many countries around the world who come together in one place to discuss important issues regarding faith and church. These large councils are known in Catholicism as ecumenical councils – from the Greek word *oikoumene* – meaning the whole inhabited world. It must be remembered that in 1,700 years ago when the first ecumenical council was called, the difficulties of travel and communication meant 'the inhabited world' was quite a small place. As mentioned earlier, small local councils, called synods were a feature of the church from the earliest days. Given that the Roman Empire was the major political force of the time, the conduct of the bishops in the early synods was influenced by the model of the Roman Senate. The church administrative divisions of dioceses and provinces that evolved were also based on the Roman political model.

The very first council called by the Christian Church was in c.50 CE. It is mentioned in the Acts of the Apostles (Acts 15:1–19). Paul and Barnabas had been on their missionary journey spreading the Good News around an area roughly matching modern-day Turkey. When they had arrived back to their base in Antioch, it happened that certain Christian Jews had travelled to Antioch and were preaching that circumcision was necessary for salvation (see Chapter Three). These preachers claimed that any Gentiles wishing to be part of the church should submit to circumcision. Paul and Barnabas had heated debates with these preachers on this issue because they believed God called all people – Jewish and Gentile – as they were. Agreement proved impossible, so Paul and Barnabas headed back to Jerusalem to discuss the matter with the apostles and elders. Even in Jerusalem, there were some among those present who believed that circumcision was necessary. Eventually, Peter stood up and told the council that God made no distinction between Jew and Gentile. Then Paul and Barnabas told of all the people who had heard the Good News they preached, and who believed in Jesus Christ as a result. Following this, James, who led the church in Jerusalem, declared that the Gentiles were not to be troubled by circumcision. It was enough that they had turned to God.

Even though it is not counted in the recognised list of councils of the Catholic Church, it bears all the hallmarks of a council. An issue arose that caused a problem locally, but had implications for the whole church (small though it was). The senior members got together and discussed the problem. They listened to various points of view among themselves. They listened to the people directly concerned – Paul and Barnabas. They then spoke on the matter themselves and finally came to a decision. The result of their decision was recorded in a document for reading to the believers back in Antioch.

To date, there have been twenty-one councils recognised as ecumenical by the Catholic Church. All are named after the place where they were held. These meetings can be with or without a pope present as happened in the early church. Although, it is highly unlikely that such a council would take place without the attendance of the pope, given that now only the pope alone can call such a council. In the past, the political leader of the day could convene a council. The emperor Constantine called the very first ecumenical council in 325 CE. His primary objective in doing this was to keep the peace in the empire. Keeping a tight grip on a large empire was not an easy task. The last thing Constantine needed was dissention and disunity among any group, and certainly not among religious groups. A dispute had arisen in the city of Alexandria in Egypt where a priest called Arius challenged his bishop on the relation of Jesus as Son of God to God the Father. Also, feelings ran very high about the calculation of the date of Easter between the Eastern (Byzantine) Church and the Western (Latin) Church. It must be remembered that the working out of Jesus' meaning for the Christian faithful was not something handed by Jesus to Simon Peter in a neat package. The early Christians had to figure it all out from scratch. At the time of the Council of Nicaea, the final shape of the New Testament had still to be decided upon.

In Alexandria feelings were running high as followers on each side of the debate became embroiled in the argument, which could at times become quite violent. Constantine was concerned that this violence, if it disintegrated into factions, would disturb the peace of the empire. So he tried to get the various parties to tolerate differences in the understanding of doctrine, but without success. Theologians can be a very argumentative lot and not easily pacified! He urged the three hundred or so bishops he gathered together to tease out a workable solution to their problems. He needed them to agree to a unifying creed so that the cohesion of his empire could be safeguarded.

Eventually, after much heated debate, and some nasty insults, the majority of those present agreed on a theological term that said that the Son (Jesus) was of the 'same substance' as the Father (God). That Jesus was True God of True God. This theological term for 'same substance' was borrowed from philosophy and was not a scriptural term. There were many bishops who signed up to the declaration, who had second thoughts afterwards. They were uneasy, to say the least, at the use of a non-scriptural term. On reflection, some bishops tried to roll back on what had been decided. This uneasiness is not an unusual feature of the aftermath of a council as people come to terms with change and with new ways of expressing doctrine.

The Council of Nicaea was very important in that it established a useful way to deal with crises in the church. It was now possible for a group of bishops to declare what the Christian teaching was on doctrinal issues. We also see the introduction of non-scriptural terms into doctrine. Greek philosophy played an ever-increasing role as philosophical terms were used in theological debates. It was at this council also that the basics of a common creed to which all Christians would give assent was established. Up to this there had been several creeds belonging to different territorial churches, but all declared belief in Jesus being of God, who died and rose again.

The next important council for understanding fundamental beliefs of the church was the Council of Constantinople held in 381 CE. It was at this council that the theology of the Holy Spirit was clarified. It was only at this point that the full divinity of the Holy Spirit was affirmed. It was at this council that the creed we know today was set down. It is commonly referred to in church as the Nicene Creed, but its full, jaw-breaking, tongue-twisting title is the Nicene-Constantinopolitan Creed!

The third critically important council was the Council of Chalcedon, convened in 451 CE. There was a council before Chalcedon in Ephesus, but a significant part of its focus was on the status of Mary, mother of Jesus. Tradition had it that she was revered as Mother of God and this was expressed widely in the liturgy. However, one bishop, Nestorius of Constantinople argued that Mary, as a human, could not be the mother of God – the all-powerful, all-knowing deity, who has existed for all time. Nestorius claimed that Mary should be known as the Mother of the Christ. This argument was not just about Mary, it also spoke to the divinity of Jesus. Were divinity and humanity two separate things? Or were divinity and humanity united in Jesus? This discussion eventually led to the Council of Chalcedon. It was at this council that the final touches to the church's fundamental beliefs about the God who is Three-in-One and One-in-Three was finally agreed upon.

The growth of the Christian community's intellectual understanding of God, of the place of Jesus and the Holy Spirit in relation to God was a slow process – four hundred and twenty years. This understanding came through discussion, dispute, prayer and, it must be said, ecclesiastical and imperial politics – some of it very nasty indeed. So dispute and disagreement in church is not a new phenomenon.

By medieval times it was obvious that reforms in the church were badly needed. Many bishops and abbots of monasteries lived like princes. Many of the clergy had concubines and there were problems of drunkenness, poor preaching, abuse of the sacraments and financial abuses. By now the Catholic Church was a political entity, ruling a sizeable portion of central Italy. It was as involved in political intrigue and strategic alliances as any monarch in Europe of the time. Many people who were totally disillusioned by the extravagance and behaviour of their bishops and clergy began to form groups of their own. Some of these groups displayed great religious fervour and because they lacked proper education, were seen as heretical.

There were four separate councils called that met in the Basilica of St John Lateran, the pope's cathedral (as Bishop of Rome). The First Lateran Council in 1123 was the first general council to be called by a pope rather than by an emperor or monarch. The Fourth Lateral Council (1215) had the greatest effect in bringing about reforms among the clergy, even though that effect was limited. The canons (laws) give some idea as to the problems that existed at the time and that needed to be remedied:

> We regretfully relate that not only certain lesser clerics but also some prelates of churches pass almost half the night in unnecessary feasting and forbidden conversation, not to mention other things, and leaving what is left of the night for sleep, they are barely roused at the dawn chorus of the birds and pass away an entire morning in a continuous state of stupor.
>
> Tanner, *Decrees of the Ecumenical Councils*, § 17

Reading the constitutions, one gets a sense of the state of the church leadership, and it does not paint a pretty picture. However, the constitutions prove a real desire to deal with the problems and restore healthy practices in church. For all of this, it was a council that spoke harshly of the Jews, forbidding them to hold public office, insisting they wear distinctive clothing so that they can be easily identified as Jews. They were forbidden to appear in public on certain Christian holy days, such as Passion Sunday. This aspect of church needs to be continually borne in mind – historically, some of the best of it and some of the worst of it have been constant travelling companions.

The Council of Constance in 1414–18 was a very interesting council, but for our purposes the next major council to consider is that of Trent. It was convened after the schism that occurred following the Reformation when Martin Luther and others split from the Catholic Church. Again, as with so much that happened down the years in church, Luther's original argument with the church authorities was about abuse of privilege concerning the sale of indulgences to raise money to rebuild St Peter's in Rome, not to create a new Christian denomination. Indulgences were promises that in exchange for money, people could get remission of the time needed to be spent in purgatory as a result of non-confessed sins. A plenary indulgence cleared the slate completely. Along with payment for the indulgence, which was regarded a sacrifice in itself, a change of heart was also required by the penitent. The sale of indulgences was not unusual in medieval church practice and, one imagines, offered a certain degree of comfort to penitents.

Luther, among others, objected to this particular sale of indulgences and how it was being preached, but he was not against indulgences *per se*. He later referred to it as 'the pious defrauding of the faithful'. As someone who never did things by halves, Luther posted his objections, his Ninety-Five Theses, in a public place. Just as a small movement of snow on a mountain can end up in a catastrophic avalanche, Luther's actions touched off a sequence of events that changed the face of Christianity. Luther's arguments were theological – everything depended on believing the truth Christ's promise of forgiveness and salvation offered freely and to all. The church did not possess a 'bank' of forgiveness and remission from which people could make 'withdrawals' for a price. If people were convinced by Luther's arguments, then there were implications for pilgrimages, special masses for the dead, shrines, images and veneration of relics. Offerings changed hands for these spiritual practices. Luther's arguments were likely to have financial implications for the people involved. Obviously, this did not make him a popular figure in Rome! Eventually, after much turbulent argument and, at times, fear for his life, Martin Luther split from the church of Rome.

The schism that resulted from Luther's exit from the Catholic Church was the second serious and permanent schism in the church. The date for the first – the Great East-West Schism is usually given as 1054, but it was not just one single event in one year. Trouble was brewing for many years and there were several issues under dispute – some were theological and others were political (it was ever thus!). Eventually, the church split into the Greek Eastern Church and the Latin Church – with each excommunicating the other.

From the middle ages, several attempts at church reform were made, some were moderately successful, such as those of Lateran IV. None, however, were successful as root and branch reforms. Following Luther's departure church reform became imperative. The church council that undertook to drive reform was the Council of Trent, the nineteenth council of the church. Even so, it still took many years to work through all the reforms necessary. The decrees of Trent together with the decisions of a special council set up by Pope Pius IV to enact these decrees became the source of canon law in the centuries that followed. As mentioned in Chapter Three, even though the Council of Trent achieved many badly needed reforms, it was also about identifying Catholicism over and against Protestantism. This created a tribalism that led to a whole new set of problems. Apart from religious division, there was political division in Europe along religious lines. However, it was not the Protestant states, which were hostile to Rome, that caused the pope most problems. The Catholic monarchs were altogether more troublesome. Monarchs of this era were absolute rulers, so continually challenged the authority of the pope, who behaved like a monarch in his own right.

The next serious challenge for the church was not political, but scientific. In the sixteenth and seventeenth centuries, the scientific revolution began and grew apace. This, in turn led to the foundation of scientific societies and the introduction of science to the universities. Out of this grew the Enlightenment, an eighteenth-century movement of intellectuals who valued and enshrined reason above all else, even faith. Those involved in the French Revolution were influenced by Enlightenment thinking. It was not long before Enlightenment thinkers began to challenge doctrines of the church. This is not to say that Christian theologians dismissed the use of reason in their theological efforts. In fact, many theologians valued rational thought, but always saw it as subordinate to faith. They used reason to explain and discuss matters of faith. Philosophy, which is all about using reasoned arguments, was considered to be the 'handmaid of theology'. Plato's and Aristotle's philosophies were the two philosophies of choice for the two most influential theologians of the church – St Augustine of Hippo and St Thomas Aquinas, respectively.

This new thinking was what might be called a paradigm shift in European thought. For the first time, intellectuals challenged the status quo. They challenged the authority of the church by challenging many doctrines, and original sin was their primary target. Why would a loving God condemn all humankind to eternal damnation because two people ate a piece of fruit? They argued that the church bullied people into thinking they were bad so that they would accept they needed the church to gain salvation. These intellectuals also challenged the rights of absolute monarchs. Up to this, in the eyes of many, the right of monarchs to rule as the absolute ruler was seen as a divine right, sanctioned by God. The Enlightenment and post-Enlightenment thinkers challenged this assumption. They argued for freedom of speech, freedom of the press and freedom of religion. And so the movement towards democracy began.

The combination of the challenge of the Enlightenment, which challenged religious claims; the French Revolution, which overthrew a Catholic monarchy; and Napoleon's military campaigns in annexing part of the Papal States, left the papacy feeling under threat. The French had even begun a programme of secularisation such as civil marriage and legal divorce in the Papal States they controlled. Given that the medieval popes had ruled as absolute monarchs, the likely effect of this monumental change was predictable. The papacy became very defensive, developing a bunker mentality. This attitude was further reinforced by yet another revolution – the industrial revolution of the nineteenth century.

The industrial revolution was a watershed in the modern world of the nineteenth century. Prior to this, the landed aristocracy and monarchy had all the wealth and power because of their land-holdings. They were great supporters of the church, often, it must be said, for political reasons as much as religious. The ordinary people were, for generations, tied to the landowner, and dependent on him for the roof over their heads. The industrial revolution allowed entrepreneurs and other capitalists to become very wealthy and create a whole new class of people – the middle classes – who enjoyed both power and prestige, normally the preserve of the ruling classes. What had traditionally been the peasantry now became urban dwellers with a means of livelihood, a working class who wanted political rights.

The notable intellectual, political and industrial revolutions of the eighteenth and nineteenth centuries, together with the political shenanigans going on in Europe at this time, left the papacy reeling. Pius IX (created 'blessed' Pius IX by John Paul II) set his face entirely against this modern development. One of the means by which he did this was through his *Syllabus of Errors.* This was a list of eighty errors that was attached to an encyclical that Pius IX issued against the modern world. Many of these 'errors' had been taken from the writings of earlier popes. Included among the eighty were condemnations of freedom of religion, freedom of conscience (described as an insanity!), freedom of the press, separation of church and state, democracy as a general principle. Error number eighty was that a pope should come to terms with modern civilisation and all its freedoms!

Oddly enough, it was in those countries, particularly the United States, which embraced democracy and broke the link between church and state that papal authority strengthened. Before this, monarchs were constantly interfering with the appointment of bishops and cardinals. Now, the political powers in the new democracies left the religious appointments to the Vatican and took no interest in them.

To add definition to his condemnation of the modern world, Pius IX decided to call a council of the church. There were many bishops delighted with this, men for whom there could not be too much papal authority. The church leaders felt besieged by the rapid developments of the modern world. Pius IX had an unspoken agenda (as many previous popes did) for this council – he wanted formal definition, a dogma, of papal infallibility. He called for his council to meet at the Vatican in December 1869. However, its work was cut short in July 1870 with the outbreak of the Franco-Prussian War. The council was deferred *sine die*. The subsequent historical events meant that the council was never reconvened. This became known as the First Vatican Council, because there was a Second Vatican Council called in 1959, the sessions of which ran 1962–1965. In fact, the first official act of the Second Vatican Council was to formally close the First Vatican Council. Chapter Eight will deal with the Second Vatican Council (also known as Vatican II), the twenty-first ecumenical council of the Catholic Church.

CHAPTER SEVEN

Infallibility

The issue of papal infallibility first raised its head in late thirteenth century. It was championed by a Franciscan, Pietro Olivi, in a twenty-year period, circa 1270–90 CE. There were many discussions prior to this on papal primacy, but papal primacy does not automatically draw infallibility in its wake. Papal primacy means that the pope has supreme jurisdictional authority over the whole Christian Church. Some scholars have tried to imply infallibility was already an accepted doctrine in the thirteenth century, even though it was not actually defined as dogma. In fact, many of the canonists (church lawyers) of the time, quite sensibly, rejected the implication that a juridical primacy meant that a pope was incapable of error. The sense of what was held at this time was that the church, as a whole, would not fail. As long as humankind exists, there will be a Christian community that holds to the truth that Jesus taught. This inability to fail applied to the church, as a Christian community, rather than to the person of the pope. But to acknowledge this inability to fail is not to say that the church has never erred. It has and it is important to admit this. If the Catholic Church lays claim to be a true church, as it does, it must retain a capacity to correct its errors honestly and openly. To correct them before they damage its credibility to proclaim the Good News, and before, in the words of one historian, 'They eat away the heart of the Christian message itself.'

The problem began, as problems often do, over an issue of sectional interest of a particular group. Not everyone may agree with this yet, when all the theological language is peeled away, that is what it is. The Franciscans were a new lay group that was set up in the early part of the thirteenth century. They were just one of several such groups that sprung up around this time as a reaction to the very worldly attitude of the church leadership. Several of these groups were regarded as heretical, and some were extreme, but the Franciscans were regarded as quite orthodox. The Franciscans received papal approval for their community and, consequently, papal protection. This was very important because their counter-cultural vow of absolute poverty would have been a challenge not appreciated by many of the aristocratic bishops and abbots of the time. Even during the lifetime of Francis there was dissention within the order on the rules of poverty. This argument continued through the century when, by the time of Pietro Olivi, there was a split into two mutually antagonistic groups. The larger group, the Conventuals, contained most of the brethren and the greater number of the respected leaders of the order. They favoured a relaxation in the very strict interpretation of the rule of poverty in order to be flexible in the service of the papacy and wider church. The smaller group, the Spirituals, to whom Olivi belonged, clung fast to the rule of absolute poverty. They believed that in this way they more truly followed the example of Jesus. Not only should they not own anything, but their use of goods should also reflect the rule of absolute poverty. For Olivi there were no loopholes! This did not endear Olivi to the several leaders of the order under whom he served.

In 1279, the reigning pope, Nicholas III, made it an official doctrine that the Franciscan way of life was the perfect way of life that Christ had revealed to the apostles. Not only that, the doctrine stated that the Franciscan rule was directly inspired by the Holy Spirit. The papal bull also covered the proper use of goods, although it did so rather vaguely, leaving it open to interpretation. So, although Olivi was mightily pleased and felt vindicated, there was enough interpretative space built into the papal bull to keep Olivi on the defensive. He wanted to ensure that no subsequent pope would undo the work of Nicholas III in relation to the papal bull on Franciscan poverty. Hence, the novel idea that a pope's teaching can be infallible and binding on all his successors. Prior to this, there was an acceptance of papal primacy in matters of jurisdiction, but popes could, and did, change the teaching of previous popes. The function of Olivi's claim of papal infallibility was to limit the pope's authority rather than exalting it. This claim was to try and ensure that a pope would be bound by, and could not change, an earlier teaching.

Over the next few centuries the popes were caught up with the continuing political battles that were part of life in Europe at this time. Occasionally, there were attempts at church reform with varying degrees of enthusiasm and very little impact. The Reformation was the event *par excellence* of the post-medieval church. Defining what Catholicism was, and what it was not, was one of the major preoccupations of the Counter-Reformation. The other preoccupation was serious root-and-branch reform of church.

By the nineteenth century, the pope as a ruling monarch was on the back foot. Political upheaval and the democratisation of Europe had proceeded apace. In Italy the political aspiration was focused on the unification of the groups of independent states, ruled by princes, into a nation state. The papal states which had comprised a sizeable portion of central Italy had been reduced to a narrow strip of land on the western coast. This reduction in the political role of the pope greatly exercised the mind of Pius IX. He saw the possession of the papal states as central to his religious vision. This possession of the 'Patrimony of Peter' was seen as a guarantee of the pope's universal ministry. Paradoxically, this issue of the papal states being subsumed into a larger unified Italy worked to the pope's benefit. He was seen as standing heroically for Christian civilisations against atheism and the rationalism of the scientific age. The loss of the papal states was seen as a threat to Catholicism and many Catholics from Europe came to defend them. Many Irishmen fought and died as part of this international brigade in a battle that was ill-advised and never had a chance of succeeding.

In discussing religious matters of this period, a new word enters the theological dictionary: *ultramontanism*. Literally, it means 'over the mountains'. It describes an attitude more than a geographical location. It describes those, clerical and lay, who from elsewhere in Europe, look 'over the mountains' to Rome for guidance and comfort. Ultramontanists held the pope in an almost mystical reverence. This period also saw the increasing 'Romanisation' of the Catholic Church. Church administration began to become ever more centralised with greater control being exercised by the Vatican. Rome, through the papal nuncios, started interfering in the local churches and those priests with strong Roman loyalties were promoted. Ultramontane piety also saw a surge in popular devotions to the saints and to the Virgin Mary. This was also the great age of Marian apparitions. By the mid-nineteenth century the arrival of railways and regular steamship travel allowed greater ease of travel. So many people flocked to sites of claimed apparitions and to Rome itself. This was also the time when cheaply printed material became widely available. Printed pictures of the pope adorned many households worldwide. A rather highly charged emotional and sentimental, and not altogether healthy veneration of the pope became part of Catholic piety. Pius IX was happy to foster this veneration and he became a type of cult-hero for many Catholics.

In 1867 Pius IX announced the convening of a general council of the church to meet at the Vatican – hence its name: the Vatican Council (later became known as the First Vatican Council or Vatican I). Ostensibly, this council was called by the pope to tackle the modern challenges that he believed were undermining the church. There was no overt mention of infallibility being part of the Council discussions. However, as the date for the opening of the Council approached (December 1869), it became obvious that the doctrine of infallibility was going to dominate the agenda. The ultramontanist bishops were determined that it would be defined at the Council. There were many bishops deeply uncomfortable about the idea of defining papal infallibility as a dogma, believing that it would be impossible to get right – that it would cause more problems than it would solve.

Within a month of the start of the Council, Pius IX dropped the idea of neutrality in the debate and weighed in behind the infallibilists. Even those who were moderately inclined towards the infallibility dogma were quite surprised by the pope's intervention. One bishop commented that the pope had professed his neutrality to the bishops when they arrived in Rome just before the Council. Then, very soon, the pope took every opportunity of impressing his views on infallibility, both in his papal audiences and through letters that found their way into the papers. The pope forbade the printing of books and pamphlets in Rome by those opposed to infallibility, but allowed those who were in favour to do so. One bishop who had his pamphlets printed in Switzerland and sent by post to Rome, had them confiscated by the Vatican police. He did not take this abuse of power lying down. He wrote a very strong letter to Cardinal Antonelli, the pope's Secretary of State, calling the confiscation of his work 'an injustice, a tyranny and an attack on the freedom of the bishops of the council who have the right to enlighten and be enlightened in such an important matter'. He then threatened that if he did not have all his printed material returned, he would have it reprinted outside Rome, as before. But this time he would collect them himself and distribute them, even if that risked being jailed. The pamphlets were handed over!

When one considers the role of the pope within the church and the allegiance bishops profess to him, the papal intervention in the debate was quite extraordinary. Apart from Pius IX's personal bias, all the key posts in the Council sessions were held by Italians. The Council bureaucracy was dominated by supporters of infallibility. There were limits on freedom of expression on the anti-infallibilist side, whether through publications or speaking at the Council. A significant number of amendments to the dogma (almost two hundred) by council participants were rejected without being put to a vote. The decks were well and truly stacked in favour of the dogma. This led, at the time of the Council, and in some historical works since, to the claim that the Council was not a truly free council. This, in turn, casts doubt over any of the decisions made there – particularly on infallibility, which was the 'neuralgic' issue of the Council. As with much in church, opinion is divided on this concept of freedom of the Council. Yet one cannot ignore the opinion of those bishops present at the Council who were against the dogma, who frequently claimed that the Council was not free.

Another aspect of this debate is the concept of majority/minority and its role in decision making. Numerically, the bishops against infallibility were significantly smaller compared to those who were pro-infallibility, they comprised approximately twenty per cent of the bishops. Yet they were leaders of about half of the world's Catholic population of the time. Also, it needs to be noted that the number of Italian bishops and those from the Oriental Rite churches made up forty-three per cent of the total bishops. These leaders, along with some missionary bishops, were dependent financially on the Holy See and were vulnerable to pressure, given that the pope had joined ranks with the infallibilists. Even though the number of bishops present at the infallibility vote was the smallest number attending at any time of the Council, the Italians and the Oriental Rites bishops, those most vulnerable to pressure, still made up approximately forty-three per cent of the total.

On the day of the vote for the infallibility dogma, 535 votes were in favour and 2 against. Many of those who opposed the dogma absented themselves, either by not being in Rome for that day, or having left altogether and gone home. About half of this group did not vote at all. Sixty-four bishops signed letters to cast their negative votes in writing, which was permitted. Yet the vote is usually regarded as having only two votes against papal infallibility. It is reasonable to ask the question why the bishops did not attend the voting session. Why did they not stay and publicly vote against the dogma? An obvious answer is that they simply did not want to be seen as voting against the pope, as creating any kind of division in church. A show of unity seemed to be very important, especially, in a wider political, scientific, philosophical and social environment that was seen, in no small part, as hostile to church.

The declaration of papal infallibility is the last part of the last document of the last session of Vatican I, and runs:

> But in this very age when the salutary effectiveness of the apostolic office is most especially needed, not a few are to be found who disparage its authority, we judge it absolutely necessary to affirm solemnly the prerogative which the only-begotten Son of God was pleased to attach to the supreme pastoral office.
>
> Therefore, faithfully adhering to the tradition received from the beginning of the Christian faith, to the glory of God our saviour, for the exaltation of the catholic religion and for the salvation of the Christian people, with the approval of the sacred council, we teach and define as a divinely revealed dogma that when the Roman pontiff speaks *ex cathedra*, that is, when, in the exercise of his office as shepherd and teacher of all Christians, in virtue of his supreme apostolic authority, he defines a doctrine concerning faith and morals to be held by the whole church, he possesses, by the divine assistance promised to him in blessed Peter, that infallibility, which the divine Redeemer willed his church to enjoy in defining doctrine concerning faith or morals. Therefore, such definitions of the Roman pontiff are of themselves, and not by the consent of the church, irreformable.
>
> So then, should anyone, which God forbid, have the temerity to reject this definition of ours: let him be anathema.
>
> Tanner, *Decrees of the Ecumenical Councils*

We have seen above that infallibility is not belonging to the tradition of the church from its inception. It was a medieval doctrine that was useful to a small number of people who just happened to have a very skilled advocate for its cause. The freedom of the bishops at the First Vatican Council was circumscribed, to say the least. Even though there was an overwhelming vote in favour of infallibility, there was not what John Henry Newman called a 'moral unanimity'. However, the more moderate supporters of infallibility managed to have sufficient influence to modify Piux IX's wish to have the pope declared infallible, and managed to focus the dogma on the teaching of the pope rather than the person of the pope.

The solemn declaration of infallible doctrine has only happened twice since 1870 – once to declare the Immaculate Conception of Mary and once to declare the Assumption of Mary into heaven. Despite this, there has been a worrying escalation of infallibility over all types of documents, which ordinarily should have varying degrees of authority. But this new infallibility is being called by another name – it is 'teaching to definitively held'. Such teaching is to be considered, even though it is not labelled 'infallible', to be irreformable. This is so, even though the teaching is not to be held as an article of faith.

This new category of 'definitive teaching' or 'teaching to be definitively held' is not the result of an ecumenical council, nor has it arisen from a comprehensive consultation with bishops around the world, nor is it the result of theological debate. It is issued from Pope John Paul II, with a commentary note by Cardinal Ratzinger. There is great concern in the theological community because of its effect on theological debate and discernment. If the label 'teaching definitively to be held' is applied, and it is with no small degree of enthusiasm, then the room for manoeuvre, for interpretation, for development or change is ever more constricted. One canon lawyer calls this 'creeping infallibility'.

CHAPTER EIGHT

Modernism

'Modernist' and 'anti-modernist' are two very charged terms in church history and carry a lot of baggage. Even though they are emotive words, these two words make the most sense in this particular context. They are used here, then, as historically understood terms. Modernists were those in church who wanted to engage theologically and philosophically with the world, while remaining rooted in their faith. Anti-modernists were those who despised anything deserving of the term 'modernism'. They were those who saw church as the 'perfect society' homogenous and linear, transcending time and beyond cultural conditioning.

What ended up being called the 'modernist crisis' was created by the anti-intellectualism of Pius X and his advisors in the early part of the twentieth century. A number of commentators have likened the situation to McCarthyism in 1950s America. The relevant Vatican documents of the period undoubtedly display a distinct paranoia. Although the condemnation of modernism may appear to have been overtaken by Vatican II, anti-modernism is still alive and well. The modernist/anti-modernist confrontation was not a single event belonging to a particular time – like so much else in church, it was more complicated than that. It was, and still is, a state of mind, and needs to be viewed as such to understand what it was all about.

Modernism was not a particular movement attempting to undermine the fundamentals of Catholicism. It was not even an organised group – it was a number of individuals with searching minds corresponding with each other through letters. Modernism was more an exploration of theological ideas and biblical study than any declaration of intent. This questioning was sparked by Leo XIII's cautious acceptance of the need for scholarly study of the bible. He had issued an encyclical called *Providentissimus Deus* (*Most Provident God*) in 1893 in the conviction that there can be no contradiction between the word of God and the sciences. God who created nature and is the author of scripture cannot contradict himself. By the early twentieth century, so much had happened in the world with the various political, scientific and industrial revolutions. Not to mention the revolution in scripture studies within Protestantism. Given its 'bunker' mentality, the Catholic Church was being left behind.

There are five names generally associated with modernism: Maurice Blondel, Alfred Loisy, Baron Freidrich Von Hügel, Lucien Laberthonnière and George Tyrrell SJ. They operated from a spirit of inquiry. Tyrrell believed 'a modernist to be a Christian of any denomination who is convinced that the essential truths of his religion and the essential truths of modern society can enter into a synthesis'. That is, Christianity, of whatever denomination, and the modern world were not incompatible. With this in mind they, variously and separately, attempted to consider:

a) biblical interpretation through the new historical-critical methods

b) revelation – both divine immanence (the God-within) and the role of the person

c) the evolution of dogmas (development of doctrine)

Some modernists explored aspects of human nature such as love, effort and will. They also gave consideration to human experience as a source of revelation. The idea of experience as a source of revelation would have been an anathema to the Catholic Church of the time. Some explored the possible connections between Catholicism and Christian democracy. Others focused on the conversation between science and religion especially regarding the

Genesis story of creation (Charles Darwin's theory of evolution had caused quite a stir since its publication in 1859). The various people described as modernists may have differed in their approach to the engagement with the modern world. Nevertheless, Tyrell's definition, in a general sense, could be attributed to those named above and their fellow-travellers. They were all committed Catholics and sincere in trying to engage their Catholicism with modern thought for the benefit of all participants in the debate. That is, apart from Loisy, whose Catholic loyalties were distinctly fluid and became even more so over time.

Following the French revolution, democracy gathered momentum in Europe. The scientific and societal changes during the nineteenth century were profound. These impinged on the church's place in the world, its material wealth and its control on people. One commentator noted that the modernists were a symbolic focus for the hierarchy's attack on what it perceived as subversive forces, which it held responsible for the church's many problems. The first strike against the modernists came with the issue of the decree *Lamentabili Sane Exitu* (*With Truly Lamentable Results*) by the Holy Office in July 1907. It condemns sixty-five propositions, fifty-three of which were derived from Loisy's writings. There was no explanation of the degree of error in each case. The ink was barely dry on that decree when the encyclical *Pascendi Dominici Gregis* (*Feeding the Lord's Flock*) was issued only two months later in September 1907.

If in 1893 *Providentissimus Deus* raised a yellow flag warning 'swim in these waters, but with care', *Pascendi* was definitely a red flag: 'Dangerous waters – no swimming allowed!' The language of *Pascendi* is harsh, intolerant and, at times, vicious. There is now a consensus that it was *Pascendi* itself that actually organised modernist thought into a system. Prior to this, it had been diverse and unorganised. It was simply a number of individuals involved writing in journals and exchanging letters. This encyclical created a straw man and then proceeded to knock him down. The writer of the encyclical, in the absence of a coherent system to attack, carefully constructs one, then attributes the existence of that system to an organised group of modernists and proceeds to assault it with venom. It accuses modernists of employing 'a very clever artifice, namely to present their doctrines without order and systematic arrangement into one whole, scattered and disjointed one from another so as to appear to be in doubt and uncertainty, while they are in reality firm and steadfast' (*DPG*, n. 4). The writer also felt impelled to rage against 'that most pernicious doctrine which would make of the laity a factor of progress in the Church' (*DPG*, n. 27).

The tone and language of the document is at times quite vicious. It becomes difficult to read, even at a remove of one hundred years, without feelings of disgust and anger.

The final and fatal blow to any hope of bringing the Catholic Church into a conversation with the modern world was delivered by the 1910 anti-modernist oath, *Sacrorum Antistitum*. This is described by one historian as 'a lengthy and ferocious oath' which was designed to 'impose a straitjacket of orthodoxy'. It wholly reaffirmed the contents of both *Lamentabili* and *Pascendi* by name. It obliged all teachers in seminaries and those being ordained to take this oath. Authority rather than reasoned argument obliterated the first real attempt by some members of the Counter-Reformation church to engage with the modern world.

The historical importance of the anti-modernist oath is in the fact that it was treated as a type of creed by the clerical church; and that it was used as a guide to the study theology by teachers of dogmatic theology. This oath, more than any other document, kept alive the memory of modernism long after modernism ceased to be seen as an actual threat. The anti-modernist oath was not an isolated action against an isolated event. It became a mindset the fruits of which, particularly in the academic theology, were a bitter harvest. Many scholars suffered dreadfully under the repressive anti-modernist regime. Some were dismissed or silenced, while compliant non-entities, of mediocre ability, were promoted. Every utterance, every piece of writing had to be parsed for signs of modernism. A secret society, encouraged by Pius X, called *Sodalitium Pianum* was set up. This group waged a particularly nasty witch-hunt until it was disbanded by the next pope, Benedict XV. Unfortunately, the spying and anonymous denunciations still continue.

As a result of the anti-modernist oath, the study of theology became very narrowly focused and paid little attention to complex historical data. This was evident in a number of important encyclicals (*Mortalium Animos* 1928, which was deeply anti-ecumenical, *Casti Connubii* 1930 against 'artificial' contraception and *Mystici Corporis* in 1943 in which the Roman Catholic Church as a visible hierarchy is identified with the mystical body of Christ). The type of theology influencing the church at this time was un-imaginative and intellectualist in its approach. It was more interested in the type of conclusions to be drawn from revealed truth than in the reality of the great mystery itself. In its own narrow little universe, the church flourished. This was achieved by its own self-imposed restricted terms of reference and by turning its back on the world. However, it could not remain hermetically sealed indefinitely within this narrow and constrained orthodoxy.

Despite the heavy burden of anti-modernist strictures that were imposed by the Vatican, many scholars continued working as best they could within the limits imposed upon them. They did so in the fields of liturgy, biblical interpretation, social action, lay partici-pation, ecumenism and the missionary movement. Though singly, none of these efforts were major events, together they were critical in preparing the ground for future growth. This potential was realised in the tragedy of World War II. In the years 1936–39 there had been much discussion by theologians on the nature and method of theology. The post-medieval, Rome-centred model of church was simply proving unworkable both in intellectual and social terms. The Catholic Church was forced to begin to look outwards again.

In some respects, given the intensity and geographical spread of the war, it seems very odd that an encyclical on biblical criticism,

Divino Afflante Spiritu (*Inspired by the Divine Spirit*) should be promulgated in 1943 right in the middle of the hostilities. Yet it was that very horror which precipitated the encyclical: 'If these things which we have said … are necessary in every age, much more urgently are they needed in our sorrowful times … when a cruel war heaps ruins upon ruins and slaughter upon slaughter' (*DAS*, n. 56). Whether it was intended to be or not, *Divino Afflante* was the net that gathered the small events which had been maturing in the previous decade. It was the impetus for *la nouvelle théologie* (the new theology) of Yves Congar and others. Congar suffered greatly at the hands of the anti-modernists in Rome but courageously held on to his vision of church. Another significant event of post-war church was the broadening of the international base of the cardinals. This was an important dilution of the influence of the formerly predominant highly conservative Italian cardinals and its effects were especially felt at Vatican II.

As always, for every small step the church makes forward there are the watchdogs of orthodoxy ready to rein it back. In 1950 the encyclical *Humani Generis* (*The Human Race*) was promulgated to put the brake on the advances set in motion by *Divino Afflante*. It looked back to Pius IX's directive that it is the function of the 'noble office of theology to show how a doctrine defined by the Church is contained in the sources of revelation … in that sense in which it has been defined by the Church.'(*HG*, n. 21) This meant that the main role of theologians was simply to explain the teaching of the magisterium. They had no role in critiquing the teachings or bringing any educated opinion to bear it. The papal document also castigates the results of biblical criticism, especially symbolic or spiritual interpretations. It calls such developments in understanding 'novelties' which have 'borne their deadly fruit in almost all branches of theology'(*HG*, n. 24). This has disturbing echoes of *Pascendi* which stated that it is necessary not just to challenge the 'open enemies' of the church but those who 'lie hid, a thing to be deeply deplored and feared, in her very bosom and heart, and are the more mischievous, the less conspicuously they appear'. And who are 'thoroughly imbued with the poisonous doctrines taught by the enemies of the Church' (*DPG*, n. 2).

Humani Generis admonishes those who question the teaching that the 'mystical body of Christ and the Roman Catholic Church are one and the same thing' and those who do not accept 'the necessity of belonging to the true Church in order to gain salvation' (*HG*, n. 27). The anti-modernist tone of *Humani Generis* slowed the pace of advances made but could not stop them entirely. If the church wanted to be relevant to the democratised, scientifically advancing, increasingly better-educated post-war world, it needed to recognise that it had to take a long hard look at itself. This it managed to do in Vatican II but not without opposition from the anti-modernist mindset within.

Vatican II is usually viewed as *the* major event of the twentieth century for the Catholic Church. However, the scandal of clerical sexual abuse of minors and its cover up has eclipsed it. Most of Vatican II's documents have significant elements that have overtaken the church's condemnation of modernism, but the reach of anti-modernism can still be easily discerned within them. Vatican II in all its major documents engaged with the modern world to great effect. However, the internal struggles that were a part of their formulations would suggest that some historical-critical analysis of the documents themselves is overdue. The ambiguity of some of the documents leaves them open to interpretations that were never intended by the majority of the Council participants. Such interpretations are freely made by those who never truly accepted the validity of the doctrinal revolution that occurred during the Council.

Paul VI abolished the Index of Forbidden Books in 1965 and he abolished the anti-modernist oath in 1967. The inherent freedoms given by these abolitions were the logical progression of Vatican II. However, the promulgation of the document on birth control, *Humanae Vitae* (*On Human Life*), in 1968 managed, in a single stroke, to undo much of the good of Vatican II. It relied on the old attitude of the imposition of authority rather than reasoned argument or sound theological foundations. Though it was not immediately obvious at the time, history has shown that this was a watershed in the church's history. This was when it truly lost credibility in the minds and hearts of a significant number of its followers. For all that, there is a general acceptance in theological circles that *Humanae Vitae* has become the litmus test of a bishop's (or a potential bishop's) loyalty (see Chapter Nine).

Though he did not reassert the place of the pre-Vatican II church during his long pontificate, John Paul II nevertheless displayed disturbing tendencies in that direction as can be seen by the following look at just some issues:

1. The promise of collegiality so hard won at the Council was virtually extinguished. It was replaced by an autocratic, monarchical style so reminiscent of Pius IX's pontificate. The implications for theology of papal favour of ultraconservative groups are worrying, as is the strategic placement worldwide of bishops who belong to these groups.

2. The anti-modernist oath may have been abolished in 1967, but a similar oath *Ad Tuendam Fidem* (1998) and its accompanying commentary from the CDF show disturbing signs of 'creeping infallibility' (see Chapter Six). The implications for theologians have been profound. An atmosphere of fear and uncertainty reasserted itself in theological institutes during John Paul II's pontificate, which has not abated. The freedom of theological inquiry so clearly affirmed in Vatican II's document *Gaudium et Spes* (*Joy and Hope*) (n. 62), and other documents, has been severely curtailed. Some outstanding theologians have suffered under the Vatican's interrogation procedures which lack the basic juridical norms of most civilised societies. These include, among other things, being able to face your accusers. Several theologians have been silenced or have had their

teaching mandates withdrawn. (Hans Küng notes in his memoir (vol. 1) that the Catholic Church is not allowed to sign the Declaration on Human Rights of the European Commission because its own inquisitorial procedures fall short on the standards required for due process.)

3. The primacy of authority, not only over reasoned argument but sound biblical exegesis too, reared its ugly head again in the issue of women's ordination. John Paul II, in *Ordinato Sacerdotalis*, declared the issue closed in 1994 by reason of his authority alone and even forbade any further discussion on the matter. Lavinia Byrne, author of *Woman at the Altar* (London: Mowbray, 1999) had stocks of her book pulped by order of the Vatican and felt obliged to leave her congregation of sisters despite her commitment to her religious vocation, to protect them from the attentions of the Vatican resulting from her writings.

4. The document *Liturgiam Authenticam* (*Authentic Liturgy*) (2001) and the later hostile takeover of ICEL (the International Commission on English in the Liturgy) by the Vatican's Congregation for Divine Worship make for disturbing reading. The result of this takeover has left us with an appalling English translation of the liturgy, which came into effect in 2011 (see Chapter Twelve).

The condemnation of modernism in 1907–10 was a particular event, but anti-modernism is a mindset that has been assiduously at work in the church throughout the twentieth century. It is now reaching into the twenty-first century also. The Second Vatican Council did not overcome this mindset; it merely left it somewhat concussed. Anti-modernism made a triumphant recovery during the Wojtyla papacy. This may yet prove a pyrrhic victory because authority, the very bedrock of anti-modernism, has been severely compromised – not by theological challenge but by the reality of clerical sexual abuse and the scandal of its cover-up by church leadership. Apart from its compromised authority, the church's very credibility as an institution has been equally compromised. But this time there may no longer be any modernist appetite to help rescue it from itself. If we have learned anything from the history of modernism/anti-modernism it is never to underestimate the tenacity, energy and utter self-righteousness of those who, in the words of Maurice Blondel 'see too clearly to see well'.

CHAPTER NINE

The Second Vatican Council

The Second Vatican Council, also known as Vatican II was called in January 1959 by John XXIII. Angelo Roncalli was an elderly bishop, who was elected as a 'caretaker' pope only three months earlier. Up to this time, all the general councils of the church were called to resolve theological and doctrinal disputes. They often included disciplinary issues, particularly regarding the clergy. They were also loaded with threats and anathemas. Vatican II is often referred to as a pastoral council. It is called such, because it was convoked to address general issues of the place of the church in the modern world, not to deal with issues of doctrine. Some of those rather ambivalent about the status of Vatican II are inclined to refer to it as 'only' a pastoral council, as if it was of a lesser order than a council convoked to deal with doctrinal disputes. The Council sat for four sessions between 1962 and 1965.

In 1959 the internal world of the church appeared very stable, not least because it had turned its back on the world following the First Vatican Council. It consolidated this isolation during the early part of the twentieth century with its 'anti-modernist' stance. Therefore, many of the curial cardinals saw no need for a council. In his book on John XXIII, Peter Hebblethwaite describes them as being 'unresponsive to his dramatic announcement. For all they appeared to care, he might have been reading out his laundry list.' The phrase associated with John XXIII and his council is *aggiornamento*. It roughly translates as 'updating'. But more than just an 'updating', the pope was deeply affected by the events of World War II, which had only ended fourteen years previously. Having spent twenty-seven years in the Vatican diplomatic corps, Bishop Angelo Roncalli was the papal nuncio to Bulgaria, to Turkey and Greece, and to France. He had experience of the world outside the clerical atmosphere of Rome and the Vatican. He had close contacts with Islam and had made many friends in his various international postings. He knew that the church must engage with the modern world because it had an important message to relate. Simply put, Vatican II was the Catholic Church coming out of the isolation of its own self-made bunker and engaging with the modern world. This it did under the guiding hand of the former Bishop Roncalli, now Pope John XXIII. Apart from the pope's own desire for *aggiornamento*, much theological ferment and biblical insights were bubbling away. These were not always appreciated by those in control, but that did not stop it happening anyway.

However unimpressed the cardinals may have been at the pope's idea of a council, a huge number of the world's bishops and other church leaders (over 2,500) attended the Council. In preparation for the Council, letters were sent to 2,598 leaders. A seventy-seven per cent response rate was returned – which by any measure is quite remarkable. The letter, which had the pope's approval, was sent to those eligible to attend as voting members – those of the rank of bishop and higher. It was also sent to the leaders of religious orders of men only – women were a scarce breed at Vatican II! In order to prepare topics for discussion at the Council, they were asked to offer their ideas and suggestions with complete freedom and honesty. Added to this, invitations to consultation were extended to institutes of higher learning that had papal charters. It may seem rather strange, given the eventual results of the Council, but the consultation by letter revealed that most respondents were in favour of the *status quo* of the church. Not only that, they wanted condemnations of various perceived 'evils' both inside and outside the church. There is a perception that the Council was a battle between the liberals and the conservatives. It is truer to say it was a struggle between the moderately conservative who were open to the world and the ultraconservative who preferred a fortress church.

Despite this initially defensive attitude, many bishops brought a theological advisor with them. It took some time for the participants in the Council to realise that they were not being called to Rome to simply rubber-stamp pre-prepared documents. They were expected to develop the documents themselves from their discussions. Eventually, by the end of the Council, sixteen documents were promulgated. They included, among others, documents on divine revelation, the church itself, the church in the modern world, liturgy, religious freedom, ecumenism, relations with non-Christians.

Reading the sixteen basic documents of Vatican II in the early twenty-first century, one is tempted to ask: what was all the fuss about? What is laid out in these documents seems quite un-remarkable if the New Testament writings underpinned one's Christianity (as they ought). That such anodyne documents caused such upheaval seems difficult to understand for someone who did not experience pre-Vatican II church. That is, of course, unless one looks into the recent history of the church prior to the Council. From Pius IX and his Syllabus of Errors and the manipulations of the First Vatican Council on papal infallibility, the intellectual asphyxiation caused by the anti-Modernism of Pius X, to the autocratic papacy of Pius XII. Set against this background it is immediately obvious that the documents are a watershed in the Catholic Church. This is because of their solid base in scripture, in their openness to the whole church of the People of God and their engagement with the modern world. In *Saints & Sinners*, Eamon Duffy says: '*Lumen Gentium* [the document on the church itself] and *Gaudiam et Spes* [the document on the church in the modern world] were great acts of theological reorientation, reshaping the parameters of Catholic theology.' Despite this advance, some would say that before the Council had been concluded, the forces of reaction had set in. However, it would be true to say that, before the Council even began, the forces of reaction did not want it to happen at all, and if it had to happen it ought to be nothing more disturbing than rubber-stamping documents that maintained the *status quo*. Hebblethwaite says: 'The process of cutting the Council down to size began on the very day it was announced.' In the USA Cardinal Spellman's immediate reaction was: 'I do not believe that the Pope wanted to convoke a Council, but was pushed into it by people who misconstrued what he said.'

Spellman and others had underestimated the resolve of John XXIII to bring the church into the twentieth century. The pope was determined to have his council. He worked tirelessly to bring it about, despite his advanced age. He was an astute man – the Italians, at the time, used the word *furbo* to describe him. It means canny, sharp-witted, astute. Though he had admitted, in private, to left-leaning tendencies, he was quite conservative on matters of doctrine. He had a very fine balancing act to maintain. It might surprise people to know that in 1961 and 1962, respectively, he put his name to a document that vigorously dealt with the primacy of the authority of the pope and a document that was intended to revitalise the use of Latin which forbade bishops to write anything against the use of Latin. In his book on the Council, Henri Fesquet noted: 'It is the practice of the Roman Church – and it is more of a strength than a weakness – to play several tunes at once. John XXIII is a flexible pope; when he gives in or remains silent on one point, it is most often because he wants to win on another which he considers more important.'

In many of the various commissions set up to organise the Council and advise the Council Fathers, conservative cardinals were given the chair. This appeared to be an effort by John XXIII to help these men participate in the renewal by giving them a significant input into the proceedings. Though they did not see the reason for a council, once its inevitability was apparent, they used their positions to their advantage. They 'stacked the decks' by dominating the commissions. They placed those they could trust in the office of presidents and secretaries and only invited 'safe' theologians to participate. However, there were increasing complaints about the commissions and their heavy-handedness. The pope then personally invited many forward-looking theologians anxious for the necessary renewal of the church to participate. The reform-minded leaders had to be constantly on guard against those who sought to undermine the work of the commissions at every turn. Xavier Rynne, in a four-volume work on the Council, offers fascinating contemporary reports of proceedings. For example, he tells us that in the preparation of the Decree on the Liturgy two German cardinals noted:

> The original document prepared by the Liturgical Commission had been altered; certain important sections dealing with the biblical foundations of the liturgy had been suppressed, while an admonition had been inserted cautioning that the schema laid down only general principles, for the application of which direct recourse must be had to the Holy See. As the speakers pointed out, this latter insertion by 'unknown hands', could strip conciliar decisions of their effect, leaving the reforms considered so essential by the bishops at the mercy of certain Roman official, as had been the case up to the present.

(Xavier Rynne was the pen-name of Fr F. X. Murphy, a Redemptorist, who was a 'mole' in the ultra conservative group. He uncovered many of their unsavoury machinations and brought them into full view in the books published under his name. The books were ghost-written by a New York book editor, John Chapin, as Murphy lacked the requisite talent for publication-standard writing.)

The safe, 'no change' documents prepared in advance by those in the Preparatory Commission, in an unprecedented action, were thrown out by the majority of Council Fathers when they began their early discussions. There seems to have been a surprise among the bishops at their new-found voices. They slowly realised that they were not there in the Vatican as a matter of form. They had a role to play – a very important role on which the very credibility of the church in the modern world depended. Many of them rose to the challenge – names like Liénart, Frings, Dopfner, Suenens, Gracias, Lercaro, König, Weber, and so forth, featured again and again, speaking so much good sense with so much passion. Reading the accounts fifty years later, one can almost sense the mounting excitement as the bishops argued, discussed and stood their ground courageously for the good of the church. Those who were not theologians allowed themselves be taught by the theologians there to advise them. One cannot but feel a profound sense of the Holy Spirit being among them.

Yet in the midst of all of this excitement a tense, continuous battle was fought. There was a constant tension between those who were open to discussion and discernment and those whose only thought seems to have been 'not an inch'. By fair means and foul, the minority struggled to gain the upper hand. Rynne tells us:

> It had always been something of a mystery as to just how the Secretary General Archbishop Felici drew up the lists of daily speakers. Theoretically all names had to be handed in well in advance but when there was need for the conservative bloc to reply on the floor to some intervention which they considered particularly dangerous or outrageous, it was noted that they had little difficulty in sandwiching in their speakers at the last minute.

Indeed many of the reform-minded bishops shared Xavier Rynne's description of Cardinal Ruffini: 'He is the kind of churchman who has forgotten nothing he was ever taught but, since becoming a teacher himself, has resisted learning anything more.'

The Second Vatican Council threw a much-needed lifeline to the best theologians the church had produced in the twentieth century. Many of these men suffered deeply at the hands of the Holy Office (formerly The Inquisition, now renamed the Congregation for the Doctrine of the Faith). They were finally allowed let their gifts of the Spirit flow over the church. It was as if a bubbling spring finally broke through the hard, packed earth and irrigated the parched land around it. However, this breakthrough by the theologians was not appreciated by many in the Holy Office whose sense of being keepers of the *depositum fidei* (the deposit of faith) was marked, more than anything, by a breathtaking arrogance. Rynne reports that 'Archbishop Parente, Assessor of the Holy Office, expressed the irritation of the Curia with the implied criticism levelled against the arch-conservatives ... "At the Holy Office we are all martyrs," he exclaimed. "We have already yielded on many points, yet this is the thanks we get!"' John XXIII's words during his opening discourse would seem to have fallen on deaf ears: 'The substance of the ancient doctrine of the deposit of faith is one thing. The way in which it is presented is another.'

This extraordinary arrogance of the members of the Holy Office is an eye-opener to anyone interested in Vatican II and its agenda of reform. When following the precepts of any church one is naturally inclined to respect what is authoritatively taught. One accepts, in good faith, the integrity, intelligence and education of those in such positions. There is an assumption that the prime motivation behind the rules and boundaries is a desire to uphold the great truth that is the foundation of life itself. It is quite shocking to come to the realisation that control, not service, was really at the heart of the church's 'authority'. In reading about what went on behind the scenes at Vatican II from various sources, one is compelled to ask: 'But where is the gospel in all of this?' It is difficult to retain respect for a teaching authority that involves itself in deceits and manipulations that were centred on the maintenance of control of the many by the few.

John XXIII was not especially liberal, nor was he highly assertive, yet he appeared to have a firm grasp on the reality of the potential damage the Holy Office was capable of doing and diffused much of this negative influence, mostly by affirming the work of the reforming bishops who gained courage under his benign watch-fulness. He showed an instinctive leadership in a very delicate situation.

Perhaps Vatican II's greatest gift to the church was the freeing of the theologians. The prophetic theologian is a blessing to the church. Of course, such people have always been problematical because they are continually testing the boundaries. They hold the church up to the gospel to check the authenticity of its message. Through history such theologians have suffered, because when the church failed in comparison with the gospel, reform of the institution was not the natural inclination. The theologian was usually the one to bear the brunt of the consequences. Only retrospectively, through the prism of history, have some of the worst-treated been valued and seen as prophetic. Happily, many of those who contributed so much to Vatican II were recognised in their lifetime. The opening up of their talents for the benefit of all God's people brought breadth and depth to the conciliar documents as they educated the bishops of the world in the various lectures organised for them. Their influence continues to the present day through their writings. Unfortunately, very little seems to have been learned from the experience – theologians are again the subject of threats and punishments for their service to the church.

With the death of John XXIII and the election of Paul VI, it seemed that the Council was in safe hands – but! – Unfortunately for the church, Pope Paul VI became known as the 'pope of buts'. Though well regarded by many, with good reason, he did not appear to have much confidence in himself or the reforms coming from the Council hall. Though he was a staunch advocate of Vatican II, it seemed that Paul VI did not have sufficient confidence in the decisions of the vast majority of the bishops. They, by now, had wholeheartedly embraced this reforming council. He allowed the 'prophets of doom' (as John XXIII called the curial cardinals) disproportionate influence and they exploited this weakness to the full. Duffy explains that Paul VI wanted that

> no one should feel steamrollered. There was to be, he declared, no one who felt conquered, only everyone convinced. To achieve this, he tried to neutralise conservative unease by

matching every reform gesture with a conservative one. In a series of deeply unpopular interventions, he watered down conciliar documents which had already been through most of the stages of conciliar debate and approval, notably the decrees on the Church and Ecumenism to accommodate conservative worries (which he himself evidently shared).

Bernard Häring alludes to this unwelcome development in one of his autobiographical works:

> Last but not least, there was an unpleasant surprise. Paul VI sent in to the Council new, far-reaching, suggested changes. It wasn't clear whether or not they came from the pope himself or if he had just passed them on. They concerned article 51 in *Gaudium et Spes*, and in particular the problem of the morality of birth control. The pope's suggestions would have altered the text approved by the great majority of the Council Fathers into its exact opposite meaning.

Given the rules laid down by the pope himself, this intervention was not permissible. Much frantic work was done which eventually resulted in the fateful compromise where Paul VI reserved the issue of birth control to a special commission. This commission had been set up by John XXIII and expanded by Paul VI, to examine the subject of population, family and births. This decision to move the discussion to the commission gets a short mention in footnote no. 14 to Chapter IV, part 2, of *Gaudium et Spes*. This innocuous little footnote indicated nothing of the disaster that the 'pope of buts' was to visit on the church in *Humanae Vitae* in 1968 (see Chapter Nine).

It is said that if we forget our history, then we are condemned to repeat it. The Second Vatican Council cannot be taken in isolation from the promulgation of *Humanae Vitae* three years later. This was the great act of weakness of leadership that sounded the death knell for the reforms of the Council. The leader of the Western Church lost confidence in himself, the bishops and ultimately in the People of God. The church leadership broke the trust of its people, lost its direction. The lack of direction, the exodus of those in priesthood and religious life, and the lack of ordered reform meant that the church went into a free fall. This then was blamed on 'reforms' of Vatican II. The fact that many of the reforms were never fully implemented in a systematic way, or were actively thwarted is often overlooked by those who regard Vatican II as a major mistake.

Yet something important did happen at Vatican II. It began a serious engagement with the world and with other faiths. It made what can only be called a paradigm shift. The church moved away from a feudal, medieval theology to one more engaged with the world. It saw the message of Christ as something for the world rather than something to be contained in a self-enclosed system. It is unique in the history of councils in that there were no anathemas. The documents are of their time and it shows. They are also the product of committees and votes and are at times repetitive and somewhat inconsistent. However, the language of the documents remains current. The language of the documents uses words of inclusion such as partnership, dialogue, collegiality and collaboration. Absent are words of threat, intimidation, exclusion, alienation and punishment. John O Malley SJ, a historian who writes on Vatican II, gives what he calls

> a simple litany of some of the elements in the change in style of the Church indicated by the council's vocabulary: from commands to invitations, from laws to ideals, from threats to persuasion, from coercion to conscience, from monologue to conversation, from ruling to serving, from withdrawn to integrated, from vertical and top-down to horizontal, from exclusion to inclusion, from hostility to friendship, from static to changing, from passive acceptance to active engagement, from prescriptive to principled, from defined to open-ended, from behaviour-modification to conversion of heart, from the dictates of the law to the dictates of conscience, from external conformity to the joyful pursuit of holiness.
>
> Schultenover, *Vatican II: Did Anything Happen?*

In this litany O'Malley sees what can be defined as the spirit of the Council. Reading the texts of the debates and seeing the voting patterns of the Council Fathers, one can agree with him.

Yet, even now the 'spirit of the Council' is under question. There is a move within the ultraconservative groups in the church to write their own studies of Vatican II and present them as the 'correct' interpretation. It is not enough for them to present a different perspective, which is normally a useful and welcome thing to do. There is a correlating tendency not just to present a case, but to attack the scholarly work produced by others well qualified in their field. This is often done with harsh language and unfair comparisons. One of the biggest difficulties for the ultraconservative groups is to accept that Vatican II represented change. For them, Vatican II is merely one more in a line of councils, in continuity with the Catholic 'tradition'. They cannot accept that it represents any kind of change or rupture with what has gone on before.

One of the most instructive ways to read about the Second Vatican Council is to read both contemporaneous accounts and the long view of historical accounts. It becomes obvious what the spirit of the Council was and obvious what an opportunity for church was lost.

CHAPTER TEN

Birth Control

There is a tendency in some church quarters to consistently link contraception and abortion. The first thing that needs to be stated here is that contraception and abortion are two very different things. When challenged on this point, those who support this connection speak then of 'a contraceptive mentality'. This is meant somehow to encompass abortion in the discussion on contraception. It is intellectually dishonest to attempt to link them in this way. They need to be separated in thought and argument so that justice is done to each.

Contraception is not a twentieth century phenomenon. There are references to it in Egyptian writings from as far back as four thousand years ago. Although one wonders at the usefulness of applying crocodile dung as a contraceptive! The Hebrew bible does not contain any rule against contraception. There is a perception that the Hebrew bible story of Onan is a scriptural basis for forbidding contraception. Onan would not, as the Law required, have full sexual relations with his widowed sister-in-law, in order to raise children in the name of his deceased brother. He practised *coitus interruptus* and 'spilled his seed'. This, according to the story, displeased God who killed him for his disobedience. It is not clear from the story why Onan refused to carry out this duty, only that he was punished for it. The punishment may have been for his disobedience to his father who ordered him to go to his sister-in-law. It may have been for his own selfishness, refusing to do his duty by his brother and the wider family. It is certainly not clear that the punishment is for what was, in effect, a contraceptive act. Given that there were not any laws against it, this would seem unlikely to be the purpose of the story. The reason Onan came to figure quite significantly in Catholic thought is that St Jerome, who in the fourth century translated the bible from Old Latin into what is now called the Vulgate, made Onan's sexual act the reason for God's punishment. Jerome used the word 'detestable' to describe the act. This is a harsh word that he does not use anywhere else in his translation. He did not get this word from his Old Latin version of the bible. He got it from a previous commentary on the bible by an earlier writer. Jerome's editing and shaping of the text to reflect his own negative judgment of the practice was to make this biblical passage a strong text against contraception.

Jerome's attitude, however unhelpful, was not altogether surprising. As early as the New Testament, the focus of best living shifted significantly to virginity. This teaching was a radical break with the Hebrew bible which fostered marriage and family as an ideal. For many of the earliest Christian writers, this focus on virginity overshadowed the teaching on marriage and placed it on the back foot, as it were. Marriage had to find justification in a way that it did not have to before this. Matters were not helped by the fact that the predominant Greek philosophy that influenced the earliest Christian writers was Stoicism. The Stoics distrusted emotion and did not admire dependence on others. They strove to control bodily desires by acts of rationality. Passions were suspect and, therefore, marriage must have some other basis for its existence; the Stoics understood this to be a necessity for the propagation of the species. This reduced the sexual act to the level of a biological function, robbing it of the affection and the expression of love that had been an integral part until then. Inherent in such a biological view was the exclusion of contraception, because it interfered with the biological purpose of the sexual act. This Stoic influence remained alive and well in Catholic teaching long after Stoicism, as a philosophy, had passed in to the realm of history.

It is very important to note here that through the centuries theologians were fascinated by, speculated on and argued about the doctrine of original sin. Attitudes towards sexuality are historically very much influenced by, and bound by, this fascination with original sin. St Augustine, in the fifth century, had a thoroughly pessimistic view of sexual intercourse. This was influenced by his time spent with a group called the Manichees. This was at a very influential period of his life, from aged eighteen to twenty-eight. The Manichees practised dualistic religion where the physical was set in opposition to the spiritual. Contraception, by using the 'safe period' was encouraged because to produce children would imprison 'sparks of divine light in soggy matter'. This influence, combined with Augustine's difficulties dealing with his own sexual impulses, has been a most unfortunate base for the church's theology of sexuality. Given that he was a theologian of extraordinary ability and scholarship, his attitudes held sway with generations of theologians, even to the present day. The great esteem in which he was held by the late-medieval theologians meant that his views dominated church practice. Based on his words alone a tradition against all forms of contraception appeared to find firm ground. Prior to Augustine's time, the negative commentary on contraception was generally in the context of promiscuous behaviour or adultery. Also, the use of 'magic' potions to avoid conception was forbidden, but that was more about the use of 'magic' than the contraception itself. After Augustine, contraception was condemned as bad in itself – as being intrinsically evil.

Up to the late Middle Ages no ecumenical council had spoken on contraception. No pope had issued an encyclical letter against contraception. However, after one of the many crises in the church involving a group called the Cathars in the twelfth century, contraception was roundly condemned. The commentators, lacking any scriptural authority for their prohibitions, sought authority in the 'tradition' of the Fathers – primarily Augustine. They branded contraception as a mortal sin, and in so doing, branded the sexual psyche of the church. There is a very impoverished theology of marriage in the church. Given this, it is not surprising to note that all writings on matters of marriage and sexuality in church have been dominated by men: men who were never married, assumed to be celibate, never had children (that we know of) and, for the most part, lived in a predominantly male-only environment.

There was a slight easing in the attitude to sex and marriage from twelfth to sixteenth century, with a movement away from Augustine. However, the rigorist attitude was reintroduced in the seventeenth century. One particularly influential cleric was Cornelius Jansen (1585–1638). He was a Belgian bishop and a moral rigorist who looked back to Augustine's theology. John T. Noonan describes Jansenism, the mindset which arose from the posthumous publication of some of Jansen's writings, as 'Augustine transported from the fifth century to the seventeenth and restored without allowance for the growth that had occurred in the Church'. Some of Jansen's propositions were condemned as heretical by Innocent X in 1653. Even though Jansenism as a way of thinking was greatly frowned upon, it was not defeated. It was particularly influential in both Belgium and France. Given that the principal colleges for the instruction of English-speaking priests were Louvain and Douai, this transplanted Augustinian rigorism translated itself to English-speaking countries.

In the late nineteenth century in Europe and the United States, groups of people began to promote the practice of birth control. In response to this, there arose opposition among various national Catholic hierarchies. By the early twentieth century, the promotion of birth control had become an international movement and a hotly debated topic. In 1930 the Lambeth Conference of the Anglican Communion lifted its ban on contraception. The Catholic response was a papal encyclical called *Casti Connubii* (*Of Chaste Marriage*) formally forbidding it. The Catholic Church was still defining itself over and against the Reformation churches. One wonders if the Anglican communion had not lifted the ban on contraception whether *Casti Connubii* would have been written. It makes implicit reference to this event, declaring that:

> the Catholic Church to whom God has entrusted the defence of the integrity and purity of morals, standing erect in the midst of the moral ruin which surrounds her … [so that] she may preserve the chastity of the nuptial union from being defiled by this foul stain.
>
> *Casti Connubii*, n. 56

Although it is likely that given the hostility of many of the bishops in Europe and the United States to contraception and the movements promoting it, some document would have emerged.

Unfortunately, over the centuries, the focus on the morality of responsible parenthood was reduced to a preoccupation with sexual activity and its purposes. Some of the commentary on sexual matters displays extraordinary ignorance. F. Hürth SJ was one of the writers of *Casti Connubii* which was issued in the name of Pius XI. He said that for a woman to experience multiple orgasms is to commit 'unnatural pollutions'.

However, it only took twenty years before there was a chink in the armour of the magisterium of the church in its attitude to contraception. In 1951, Pius XII, speaking to midwives, advocated the use of the rhythm method (also known as the safe period) when there was good reason to use it. The language moved from a negative railing against contraception in any guise to a more positive 'regulation' of births. This was a tacit recognition that there might be sound medical, economic and social reasons for doing so. The church, then, had moved from outright prohibition of the safe period, to a cautious suggestion of its use to avoid *coitus interruptus*, to a guarded popularisation of it, to outright approval of it. Change happens!

It is hardly surprising that the issue of birth control did not go away. Not only was there an increasingly educated population in both Europe and the United States, but the contraceptive pill had arrived. By the late 1950s there was a newly emerging well-educated laity in the church which was beginning to have confidence in itself and to understand that the lived experience of married couples mattered. By this time, a progressive bishop in Belgium, Leo Suenens, was also organising informal conferences on the issue. In 1961 a call for the church to change its attitude to contraception came from a surprising place: *Good Houskeeping* magazine! One of the physicians who helped develop the pill, John Rock, argued that the pill only allows humans to do predictably, through their use of reason, what the body did unpredictably through the mechanism of its organs. Unsurprisingly, Rock's article invited quite a storm of reaction from the church authorities, mostly negative. But the conversation had started.

In 1963 a Dutch bishop, William Bekkers, spoke on national television. He said that the church does not have the answers on these complicated issues of birth control and the means by which to achieve it, and it should stop pretending that it does. He suggested that couples should rely on their common sense and experience:

> From within their human experience of marriage, that is, out of their lives and responsibility for each other, for their reproductive powers, and for the family that already exists, the married couple – and they alone – can answer the question of what God requires of them concretely in their vocation. They must decide how large their family should be and how their children should be spaced ... This is a matter for their own consciences with which nobody should interfere ... The Church does not judge situations from a prejudiced, aloof point of view ... It knows that what may be attainable for one person is not necessarily so for another.

Within a few months, the Dutch national hierarchy issued a statement on the pill, and they agreed with Bekkers. They stated that scientific advances had presented problems for the church and that the church had 'no immediately appropriate answers ready that meet all situations'.

Also in 1963 Suenens (by now a cardinal) urged John XXIII to form a commission to study the birth control issue in detail. He had concerns about a particular theologian, Fr Ermenegildo Lio. Fr Lio together with Fr Hürth, had submitted a draft document, *De Castitate, Virginitate, Matrimonio, Familia* (*Of Chastity, Virginity, Marriage and Family*) (See Häring, 1992 & Valsecchi), on Christian marriage for consideration at the Vatican Council. This document stated: 'It is forbidden to maintain that love is essential to marriage.' Fr Lio's reactionary writings on marriage were simply restatements of Piux XI's and Pius XII's doctrine and took no account of the development of thought about marriage that had occurred in the intervening years. This document ran the risk of slipping through the screening committees and gaining the authority of a council document. Suenens also argued that the time was ripe to present 'an intelligent position on responsible parenthood and at least try to reform the old idea – the more children the better'. An added impetus was the upcoming conference on world population problems planned by the UN and the WHO.

The pope agreed with Suenens. The Pontifical Commission for the Study of Population, Family and Births was established in March 1963, three months after the conclusion of the first session of Vatican II. The formation of the Commission was kept secret at the beginning. There were six members, all men. Four were laymen, all married, two were priests. They included two medical doctors, a demographer, an economist, a sociologist and a diplomat. There were no theologians. By the time the Commission held its first meeting in October 1963, John XXIII had died and Paul VI was the new pope.

The focus of the Commission was mainly on world population and attendant problems, but it naturally raised the issue of birth control. After its first session the group had neither disagreement nor dissent with existent church teaching on contraception. They produced quite a tame, orthodox document. In his book *Turning*

Point, Robert McClory summarises the recommendations of the group:

- Rhythm is unquestionably 'the Christian position' on family limitation, and it is hoped that modern science will develop methods 'that could be harmonized with the needs of human love and human morality'.

- Rather than wait for the Vatican Council to issue a statement on birth control, the pope himself should provide 'light and order' as soon as possible for those who are disturbed and thus help clear up confusion caused by promoters of 'the most adventuresome methods'.

- Earlier papal statements on the evils of contraception, especially those by Pius XII, constitute 'luminous teachings' and should be widely promulgated to deter overpopulated nations from promoting sterilisation, contraception, and abortion. If the church remains silent, it will fail in its role as 'defender of the natural moral law'.

- More study is needed to determine the mechanics and side effects of the pill. It would be 'preferable' for the pope not to take an absolutely definitive position on the pill at this time.

This report, with its recommendations, gives no hint of what was really happening within the church at that time. There was a widespread dissatisfaction among practising Catholics in Europe. Bishop Bekkers, the first bishop to publicly speak of change on the issue, said in a later interview that because bishops appear to speak with one voice on current church teaching, it is not necessarily consensus, it 'may be a mere slavish and subservient parroting of the pope's words'.

It was very clear – this issue was not going away. Paul VI approved a second session for the Commission to meet in April 1964. He expanded the group by adding seven new members. Five of the seven were priest theologians, two were laymen – a sociologist and a demographer, and still no women. One of the theologians, Fr Bernard Häring, was well known for rather liberal tendencies, but more than that, Häring was a supremely pastoral man. He saw beyond the rules to the people. While some theologians spoke the language of philosophy about means and ends, about sperm and ova, Häring spoke of the critical importance of love. The conclusions of this second meeting were somewhat less definite than the first, listed above.

More and more, the issue of contraception became newsworthy. Given that the debates of Vatican II were getting unprecedented press coverage anyway, this is hardly surprising. The third meeting of the Commission set for June 1964 had two new members added – two more priests, one a theologian and one a close friend of the pope. The committee now had fifteen people, ten priests and five laymen – still no women. Up to now the Commission saw itself in an advisory role. Pope Paul VI, becoming quite anxious about the whole issue, raised the stakes considerably and gave them three questions to answer:

1. What is the relationship of the primary and secondary ends of marriage? (Up to now, procreation was seen as the primary end, and the good of the couple, secondary.)

2. What are the major responsibilities of married couples?

3. How do rhythm method and the pill relate to responsible parenthood?

The members of the Commission took on this challenge, but not without a sense of uncertainty. After three days of discussion, everything was still in a state of flux and not one of the pope's questions had been answered. It seemed as if many members of the committee did not know what to do with the freedom they were given to think independently. One of the members, Thomas Burch, a married man and father of three children found himself becoming impatient. He said the more they looked at the problems of world poverty and considered marriage and the rearing of children, the attempt to operate out of the old theology looked silly.

During the 1960s there was a sustained rise in the voices of those directly affected by birth control – the lay people. John Henry Newman's essay *On Consulting the Faithful in Matters of Doctrine* (see Chapter Four) was cited several times in the debate. The issue was gaining significant momentum. For the fourth meeting of the Commission in March 1965 the membership was greatly expanded, forty-three new members were added, bringing the total to fifty-eight – thirty-five of whom were priests and twenty-three, lay people. This time there were four women present, one present as a professional demographer; two women were present with their husbands because the husbands were invited to participate in the Commission as doctors, so they were not invited as married couples per se. The fourth women was Patty Crowley, from the United States, who, with her husband, Pat, were the only couple to be invited exclusively because they were a married couple.

The Crowleys had been deeply involved in an international organisation called the Christian Family Movement (CFM). They assumed that was why they were selected. After taking some advice, they decided to notify the American national executive of the CFM about their appointment. They asked the executive to invite opinions from members throughout the country. They also put word out to their extensive range of personal contacts. Within weeks, the letters and notes piled in. The suffering and hardship that couples were enduring trying to obey the current church teaching on birth control was immense. The Crowleys selected more than a hundred of these letters to bring with them when going to Rome.

The participants at the forth meeting in 1965 were divided into three groups: theologians and historians in one group, doctors and psychologists in a second group and demographers, sociologists and economists in the third group. Being the only married couple present *as* a married couple, the Crowleys did not fit into any group – one wonders if anyone present grasped the irony of this! The other two couples fit into the medical group because of the professions of the husbands. As it happened, the Crowleys ended up in the theologians' group.

One of the most significant inputs of this session was a two-hour lecture by John T. Noonan (mentioned above) on the history of contraception. In it he showed how love, sex and marriage were understood in different historical times. He showed how doctrine could, and did, change over time and within culture. This went to the heart of the deliberations of the Commission – could doctrine change? If it could not, then there was nothing more to be said. One hard-line Jesuit member, Fr Zalba, insisted that the current doctrine was not only irreformable, but also infallible. Others argued that only matters pertaining to revelation could be considered infallible. Moral issues do not lend themselves to unchangeable judgments. And so the arguments went on. What is most interesting is to see how minds changed during the discussions. The more that people listened to the reality of the difficulties of the rhythm method of contraception, the more they allowed themselves to be open to change. Apart from John T. Noonan's lecture, a very significant influence on the group was the correspondence from members of the CFM that the Crowleys brought with them. Instead of theory, philosophical concepts, notions of irreformable or infallible doctrines, the real stories of the hardships of real people managed to be heard. This report had such an impact, the Crowleys were asked to prepare a larger and more scientific survey through the CFM for the next meeting of the Commission.

When the members of the Commission met Paul VI on the last day of their 1965 meeting, he urged them to continue their deliberations. In the light of what transpired afterwards, it is worth quoting from part of the address from the pope. The pope wanted the Commission to continue its work

in complete objectivity and liberty of spirit … You are at a new and decisive stage in your work … Give yourselves to your task wholeheartedly, let that which needs it, ripen, but listen to the anxiety of so many souls and work diligently without

111

worrying about criticism and difficulties … It is our wish that the basis of your investigations should become broader, that the different currents of theological thought be better represented in it, that the countries which know … serious difficulties … should raise their voice among you, and that laymen [sic], and especially married couples, should have their qualified representatives in such a serious undertaking.

McClory, *Turning Point*

Back home and in preparation for the next, and final, meeting in 1966, the Crowleys, with some professional help, set about producing a more scholarly, scientific report. This was to find out what life was like for couples attempting to operate the rhythm method of contraception. New questionnaires were sent out to members of CFM worldwide. Apart from the standard questions one might expect from such a questionnaire (biographical details, whether the rhythm method was used, whether it worked, whether it failed, and if it failed, why it failed), respondents were also asked questions about the effects of the method on the marital relationship. The Crowleys received approximately three thousand replies across eighteen countries. The information was gathered into a twenty-three page report for the final meeting of the Commission. There was plenty of advice for the church leadership in general, and the pope in particular, from the respondents to the Crowley survey. To quote just one:

The statements on this subject therefore must come from those who live in the situation on a daily basis. Secondhand knowledge is not adequate to serve as the foundation upon which this important area can be discussed … The Church, working together with married couples and listening to suggestions with an open mind, can prove to be the leading force in this matter. Strict laws, however, seem inappropriate and detrimental to marriage.

McClory, *Turning Point*

The final meeting of the Commission took place in early April 1966. Although not everyone present realised it at the time, the rules had changed. Without notification or consultation, the Commission members were no longer 'members' but *periti* (Latin: experts). The actual members of the Commission were sixteen cardinals and bishops were named by Paul VI to attend the final plenary meeting. For most of these men this final meeting was the only encounter they had with the Commission. Despite their lack of engagement with the whole process, it would be these sixteen, and not the fifty-eight, who would advise the pope.

At the final meeting the four women present were asked to speak to the assembled group. Nervous, but undaunted, they left those present in no doubt that change was necessary. It is interesting to note that from the first meeting in 1963 to the final meeting in 1966, minds had changed. Changed from thinking the doctrine was not reformable to believing that not only was reform possible, but necessary. Apart from the theological discussions which helped pave the way for change, the witness of so many Catholic couples for whom their Catholicism was deeply important.

Unfortunately, there were a small number of theologians in the Commission who could not accept the possibility of change. They were very concerned about the response of the Commission to the three questions posed by Paul VI. One of these, Fr John Ford SJ, without any authority from the pope or the Commission, arranged for a young professor of philosophy to be flown in from the United States. They sequestered themselves in a hotel, where they worked intensely for a week to produce a document which was presented to the Commission. This document defended the existing position on birth control in the strongest terms, at times quite aggressively. The document was signed by Fr Ford SJ and three other members, Frs Visser CSsR, Zalba SJ and de Lestapis SJ. During the final debates on the issue it became apparent that change was in the air. This was despite the fact that a majority of the members (now all clerics) were quite conservative in their leanings. Some of those present, who could not handle the possibility of change, became quite agitated. They said that a change in doctrine would endanger the idea of the church's perfection in holding the truth. This would mean that the 'gates of Hell' had in some way prevailed against the church – the very thing Jesus said would not happen. Fr Zalba was in agreement with this, 'What then,' he asked, 'with the millions we have sent to hell if these norms were not valid?' Patty Crowley's response was not only apt but delightful: 'Fr Zalba, do you really believe that God has carried out all your orders?' (McClory)

The unilateral act of Fr Ford in presenting his paper caused problems for the Commission. The 'minority' theologians refused to compromise. The cardinals and bishops had then to decide should they present two reports – a majority and a minority. It was finally decided that only one report should be submitted, the majority report – two reports would only create problems for the pope. However, the position of the minority would be taken into account and be stated in the single report. When the final report was prepared, there was no input from the minority group, because this group did not want to have anything to do with it. The final report was passed by a majority of the Commission and was its *only* official report. There was no 'minority report' authorised or produced by the Commission. The voting of the Commission on the issues was as follows:

1. Is contraception intrinsically evil?
   9 voted 'No', 3 voted 'Yes' and 3 abstained.

2. Is contraception, as defined by the majority report, in basic continuity with the tradition and the declarations of the magisterium?
   9 voted 'Yes', 5 voted 'No' and 1 abstained.

3. Should the magisterium speak on this question as soon as possible?
   14 voted 'Yes', 1 voted 'No'.

The Commission had finished its work and was disbanded. Three days later, its official report was presented to Paul VI on 28 June 1966. Unfortunately, the small 'minority group' and its followers could not accept the democratic report of the Commission. This was despite the fact that the report that was the result of a long, educative, searching and reflective process. This small group, having refused input of their views into the final report, started working behind the scenes to produce an unauthorized 'minority' report. This report had no standing and was little more than the document signed by Fr Ford and three others and presented as a working paper to the Commission earlier in the year. Cardinal Ottaviani, the head of the Congregation for the Doctrine of the Faith, the second most powerful person in the Vatican after the pope, then presented this document to Paul VI, as a 'minority report' repudiating what the majority had decided.

The pope was favourably impressed by the official commission's report, but came under intense pressure by Cardinal Ottaviani and the Franciscan Fr Lio (see above) who was a special advisor to Ottaviani. According to a comment by Fr Lio to a fellow priest, Paul VI was 'reconverted'. Häring, in his autobiographical work *My Witness for the Church*, tells us that the four dissenting theologians admitted that they could not give a convincing argument against the ban on contraceptive methods other than the rhythm method – it all came down to an issue of authority – the church could not be wrong. According to Häring, who was present at almost all the discussion of the Commission, 'Ford above all emphasized a fundamental motive: It is unthinkable that the Holy Spirit should have been more with the Anglican bishops in 1930 than with the Roman Church – unthinkable, therefore, that, after all, the Catholic Church could accept what the Anglican bishops had taught in 1930, to the irritation of Rome.' Of all the intelligent and informed debate that took place over three years involving people from many disciplines, this attitude of Fr Ford SJ, was the one that managed to win in the end.

Sadly, this tiny group won their battle, but lost the war – they damaged the church's credibility to teach with authority. Two years after the presentation of the Commission's report in 1968, Paul VI promulgated the encyclical *Humanae Vitae* (*On Human Life*). In ignoring the advice of the report of the Commission he created the biggest credibility problem the modern church had known until then. (The more recent scandalous revelations on clerical sexual abuse of children and its cover up by bishops have eclipsed everything.)

Humanae Vitae condemned 'artificial' birth control. (The catechism of the Catholic Church went a step further when it declared it 'intrinsically evil'.) When the encyclical was announced at a press conference, the bishop tasked with the job stated that the pope did not see the encyclical as an infallible and irreformable dogma. However, the 'creeping infallibility' that has become such an insidious presence in the church at present, would have it that *Humanae Vitae* is irreformable.

According to Bernard Häring, 'the encyclical hit the world like a comet – all the more so because this was not the decision generally expected.' Given his prominent place during all the deliberations, Häring knew that he would be besieged with questions and requests for comment on the encyclical and went to a convent in California for a private retreat. He did not want to find himself in public opposition to the pope. However, when he read that a prominent cardinal, Pericles Felici, was quoted in the Vatican newspaper *L'Osservatore Romano* as saying that 'whoever is unwilling to accept the norm of *Humanae Vitae* should leave the Church' Häring stood up to be counted. His response, in a nutshell, was: all Catholics had to sincerely examine themselves to see if, in conscience, they could accept the norms of *Humanae Vitae*; if they could, then they were obliged to do so. However, if after thorough reflection, they found they could not, they should also follow their conscience, but this decision was no reason to leave the church.

One of the most profound influences on the Commission was the response of married couples trying to abide by church teaching in the matter of birth control. The stress and hardships experienced were clearly stated in the Crowley survey for anyone willing to hear. When one reads the Pastoral Directive in *Humanae Vitae* on 'mastery of self', it becomes obvious that the lived experience of couples trying to live decent lives as Catholics had no value in contributing to the encyclical:

> For if with the aid of reason and of free-will they are to control their natural drives, there can be no doubt at all of the need for self-denial. Only then will the expression of love, particular to married life, conform to the right order. And this is especially true as regards the practice of periodic continence. But self-discipline of this kind is a shining witness to the chastity of husband and wife and, so far from being a hindrance to their love of one another, transforms it by giving it a more truly human character. And if this self-discipline does demand that they persevere in their purpose and efforts, it has at the same time the salutary effect of enabling husband and wife to develop to the full their personalities and be enriched with spiritual blessings. For it brings to family life abundant fruits of tranquility and peace. It helps solving difficulties of other kinds. It fosters in husband and wife thoughtfulness and loving consideration of one another.
>
> *Humanae Vitae*, n. 21

An interesting footnote to the birth control commission and its ill-fated report is that one of the sixteen bishops and cardinals named as the members of the Commission for the fifth and final meeting was a Polish archbishop, Karol Wojtyla (Pope John Paul II). Archbishop Wojtyla was absent from this final decisive meeting which lasted around three months. He did not attend as a protest against the Polish authorities who refused to let Primate Cardinal Stefan Wyszynski leave the country to attend the Vatican Council.

Unfortunately, according to Häring, his lack of attendance did not prevent him from influencing Paul VI to take the direction he did in *Humanae Vitae*. As pope, John Paul II made *Humanae Vitae* a central pillar of his stance on marriage and the family. It is accepted by many informed commentators that he also used fidelity to *Humanae Vitae* as one of the standards by which he appointed bishops.

CHAPTER ELEVEN

Canon Law

When the scale and extent of the cover-up of clerical sexual abuse became public knowledge, the words 'canon law' became part of the discussion. There appeared to be a degree of ambiguity in the minds of some people about the place and role of canon law in church. There were also questions about how canon law influences the church as it relates to society at large. Some had the mistaken view that canon law was above and beyond state law, having an almost sacred status.

The word 'canon' is derived from the Greek word *kanon* meaning measuring stick – a rule used by masons and carpenters. From that, it came to mean a rule or standard – a way of determining proper measurement. We speak, for example, of the canon of scripture. By this we mean those books of scripture we regard to be the standard for defining what is to be accepted as orthodox in our religious beliefs and practices. The decisions of the early councils were recorded as 'canons'. These were rules and regulations that were agreed upon after much debate and discussion. We do not have an official written record of the deliberations of the first ecumenical council of Nicaea, but we do have the canons that resulted. Through them we get a good idea of what was discussed. The issues were mainly about clergy discipline, conflicts of jurisdictions, the movement of bishops from one see to another and issues of apostasy among the faithful. Apostasy is where they turned away from Christianity under persecution.

Canon no. 3 from Nicaea tells us that the 'great synod absolutely forbids a bishop, presbyter, deacon or any of the clergy to keep a woman who has been brought in to live with him, with the exception of course of his mother or sister or aunt, or of any person who is above suspicion'. The only reason there would be need to forbid something is because it was already happening!

Rules and laws are a necessary part of any organisation so that it can function properly. Problems tend to arise when people attribute a status to laws and rules that gives them an existence apart from the community. It should never be forgotten that the laws and rules of an organisation are made *by* people *for* people. They are meant to serve the community; the community does not exist to serve the laws. The rules and laws of a social group are a human invention. (This is not the place to begin a discussion on the laws of physics!) Jesus, in his preaching, was very clear on the proper place of rules – they had their place, but they should never interfere with doing the right thing.

Canon law is most significantly developed in Roman Catholicism, but it has an important role in other Christian churches. This is true of both the Eastern Orthodox and Anglican Church. Some smaller Christian churches and congregations may not have a highly developed set of laws to compare with canon law, but nevertheless have books of disciplines or rules.

If it were capable of simply abiding by the teaching of Jesus, the early church would not have needed a complex set of laws and rules. It is hardly surprising, given the human capacity for conflict, this was not possible. Hence, like any group or social organisation, sets of rules developed to allow orderly functioning of the group. One of the earliest documents, dating from c.100 CE gives sets of instructions for the community. These relate to the administration of baptism, about fasting and the prayers to be said at the shared meal on the Christian Sabbath. About one hundred and twenty years later another document was produced that gave information about the ordination of bishops, priests and deacons. As time passed, other collections of documents were gathered. As the church continued to grow, it needed to meet the challenges of the times and cultures in which it found itself. It was out of the necessity to meet these challenges that we had the first synods of bishops meeting. In the early part of the fourth century CE, there were five synods held in what is now modern-day Turkey and in Syria. The decisions (canons) of these Eastern regional councils were eventually gathered into one collection towards the end of the fourth century. This was the kernel of what was to become canon law.

Latin translations of this collection of Eastern canons began to circulate almost immediately in the Western Church. Eventually the pope of the time summoned a monk called Dionysius Exiguus to come to Rome to make an accurate and complete translation of the canons. Dionysius also gathered a collection of papal letters that had been issued over the previous hundred years. These letters were called decretals. They were usually a response by the pope to a particular question put to him. These were often on a matter of ecclesiastical discipline. These decretals were meant to be the last word on the particular issue, and compliance with them was expected.

This collection of decretals made by Dionysius was a parallel collection to the canons from synods and councils. In doing this, Dionysius helped to put papal directives on an equal footing with the decisions of councils of bishops and the decretals became a constituent part of canon law. By the middle ages, the decretals were, by far, the greater part of the law. The combination of conciliar canons and decretals formed the most important body of church law during the first thousand years of its existence.

The focus in the first millennium of the church had been on collecting and preserving the writings of the past. By the twelfth century CE, as might be imagined, quite an amount of church writings had been amassed. There was a great thirst for learning. This was also the time of the development of the 'schools', which evolved into what we now call universities. The church was very well established across Europe and had the time and space to begin to consolidate and analyse the body of writings that had been collected. There were the scriptures, of course. There were also the writings of the early Church Fathers and the large collection of legal texts. It is hardly surprising that when these writings were considered and analysed, plenty of inconsistencies and, at times, outright contradictions were found among them. A method of reconciling and interpreting the texts needed to be developed. This was duly undertaken by a number of churchmen. One of them, Peter Abelard, developed a method called *Sic et Non* – Yes and No. He gathered the opinions of a number of the early Church Fathers on various theological issues. From these, he took 150 quotations and assembled a set of arguments for and against each topic.

This method of theological harmonisations of Abelard was taken up by Gratian, a canon lawyer of the time. He applied it to canon law. He wanted to gather the whole legal tradition of the church into one volume and, like Abelard, reconcile the discrepancies, inconsistencies and contradictions. In doing this, he also drew on citations from civil law. In the middle ages, a significant work of Roman imperial law, the *Digest of Justinian* was revived, and a number of Roman law texts were included in Gratian's work. In later centuries, though, this Roman law was to have a much greater influence on canon law.

Gratian's method was to take an issue, cite all the texts favouring that issue on one side, all the texts against the issue on the other side, and then conclude with his own solution. Gratian made significant use of the work done by his predecessors on this harmonisation. Even so, the body of work he subsequently published earned him the title 'Father of Canon Law'. This impressive work of Gratian, published in 1140 CE was called the *Decretum*. The publication of this work is considered to be responsible for the divergence of theology and canon law, with canon law being taught as a separate subject from then on.

The study of canon law became quite exciting, and many scholars started developing commentaries on Gratian's work, to explain what was meant by this text or that. Over the next few decades a number of skilled canon lawyers were elected to the papacy. As disputes arose over what was meant by any given text, popes, who were also canon lawyers, issued hundreds of decretals. These settled disputed points of law and provided for situations that had not existed when Gratian compiled his work. As time went on, there were more and more additions to the body of canon law. Then collections of this additional work were organised and reorganised into several books. By the early 1500s, the body of medieval canon law was fixed and remained so until 1917. Obviously, during this four hundred year stretch, there were many supplements and additions. Apart from whatever was issued from the reigning pope, a lot of material was issued from the various departments of the Roman Curia.

By the First Vatican Council, there was an overwhelming amount of law scattered over numerous publications. It was unwieldy and difficult to know what laws were valid and what were obsolete. Many bishops asked the pope to prepare a new code of canon law. Given all the political problems around the time of Vatican I, it was 1904 before a revision of the code could be undertaken. It took almost fourteen years for a large group of researchers to bring the project to fruition.

The 1917 code was modelled on the civil codes of Europe, starting with the Napoleonic Code. Prior to the French Revolution, different laws applied in different parts of France. In 1804, Napoleon enacted a systematic legal code, so the country had its first set of coherent laws that applied throughout the territory. Among other things, this code enhanced the rights of men over their families and diminished the individual rights of women. The code formed the basis of similar systems that were subsequently enacted in other European countries. The Roman Catholic Church also used the *Code Napoléon* as a model for its own revised code. By the Second Vatican Council, less than fifty years later, there was already a need to further revise the 1917 code.

Traditionally, canon law contained material from the actual social situation from which it arose and that acted as a sort of case law. However, the new revised code became almost like a set of abstract mathematical formulae to be applied as principles, set apart from the lived reality of people's lives. A code of laws as principles are useful, but how they are interpreted is vitally important. A wise and prudent interpretation of the law helps it to work. A rigid, literal interpretation can be cruel, heartless and reflect poorly on the law itself. This diminishes respect for the law among those for whom it is meant to be an instrument of good order and discernment.

In the years between the 1917 code and 1962, five volumes of new legislation were added to body of church law. When John XXIII called his council, he also indicated that a revision of the 1917 code was something he wanted as part of his *aggiornamento*. However, given the changes in the church's understanding of itself during the Council, it became obvious that any revision of the code would need to wait until after it had completed its deliberations and issued all its documents. So it was just as the Council was closing that a commission was set up to revise the code of canon law. A number of principles were agreed upon to guide the revision. Among these were: canon law should avoid excessive rigidity, those with pastoral care should have discretion in the application of the law; the principle of subsidiarity be recognised, leaving plenty of 'wriggle room' for local and regional legislation; ecclesiastical penalties should be kept to a minimum and the code should be revised and restructured in conformity with the decrees of Vatican II. The new revised code of canon law was promulgated in 1983.

As with the previous organised volumes of canon law, in the time since its publication there have been many additions and modifications to the code. One that disturbed many canon lawyers and theologians was a twofold change that happened in 1989 and

1998. But we need to step back to 1967 first. In 1967 Paul VI abolished the anti-modernist oath (see Chapter Seven). He had sufficient confidence in the profession of faith that was required to be made by those in leadership and teaching positions in church. This profession of faith was the Nicene Creed to which was added a new paragraph which clearly referred to the teachings of Vatican II. It laid a responsibility on those with ecclesiastical leadership and those with teaching responsibilities to, among other things, 'firmly embrace and accept all and everything which has been either defined by the church's solemn deliberations or affirmed and declared by its ordinary magisterium concerning the doctrine of faith and morals'. It is not a huge leap of imagination to assume that Paul VI was trying to copper-fasten the reforms of Vatican II in the face of a small, but highly influential and very determined, group of churchmen intent on rolling back the developments.

Canon 833 of the code of canon law lists those who are required to make this 1967 profession of faith. They are clergy of senior and administrative rank, professors of theology and philosophy in seminaries, deacons, and 'those who in any universities teach subjects which deal with faith or morals'.

In 1989, Paul VI's addition to the Creed was removed and replaced by a new insertion. The new text contained some material related to two existing canons in the 1983 code of canon law (750 and 752). One paragraph, however, was completely new and, to all intents and purposes, introduced a new oath of fidelity for those in the roles mentioned above in Canon 833. Though this oath lacks the ferocity of the anti-modernist oath, why an oath of fidelity was considered necessary, in addition to a sincere profession of faith, is difficult to understand.

Then in 1998 a new paragraph was added to the existing Canon 750. This canon relates to the church community at large, and lays down that Roman Catholics are obliged to believe the deposit of faith found in scripture and tradition and as taught by the teaching office of the church. This obligation is applied to all the faithful, not just clerics. The new addition to Canon 750 arose from a letter of John Paul II (*Ad Tuendam Fidem*) and runs as follows:

> Each and every thing which is proposed definitively by the magisterium of the Church concerning the doctrine of the faith or morals, that is, each and every thing which is required to safeguard reverently and to expound faithfully the same deposit of faith, is also to be firmly embraced and retained; therefore, one who rejects those propositions which are to be held definitively is opposed to the doctrine of the Catholic Church.
>
> *Code of Canon Law*, Canon 750, §2

Those canon lawyers concerned by this new addition, which applies to all members of church, point to the terms used in it. These are: *proposed definitively* and *to be held definitively*. These terms are widely seen as a 'creeping infallibility', the attempt to give the character of infallibility to teachings that do not meet the standards for infallibility as defined by the First Vatican Council.

Given that they are the result of human debate and deliberation, laws are fallible. Mistakes are made. Situations arise that could not have been anticipated when the laws were made. All laws are applied by people – they do not have an existence separate from those who made them and those who apply and enforce them. Therefore, the attitudes of those who enforce the laws influence the effects of the law on others. A person with little or no imagination, with the type of personality that is highly rule-orientated, who rarely mixes socially and who keeps within his or her own tight group will apply the law one way. The person with a good imagination, widely read, with a broad spectrum of friends and acquaintances, who sees rules more as a tool for good order than absolutes, will apply the law another way. If one is going to pass judgment on another, a rigorous self-knowledge would seem to be an important prerequisite.

So what is the role of canon law in the church? Is it just about order and control? Is it analogous to civil law, applied in the ecclesiastical setting? Like much else in church, it is a case of 'yes and no'. There are different interpretations. One of the least helpful is where canon law is aligned with faith, thus making it a rule of faith rather than a rule of reason. In this type of thinking, canon law becomes similar to dogma, and takes little account of the human nature of the church. This view also does not take into account the limitations and errors inherent in laws that are a human construction. It also lends itself to a very rigid, inhumane interpretation of the law. To balance this, there is an interpretation that runs the risk of leaning too far in the opposite direction. Such a view sees canon law as part of the sacramental structure of the church, and as a symbol of humanity being redeemed. This is to ask rather a lot of the law.

Certainly, canon law is about order and control (and I use these terms in their most benign sense here), but in the faith community it is also so much more. Faith plays a part. There is an interplay between theology and the law. The Christian community comes together because of its belief in the risen Christ. But all communities need structure to a greater or lesser extent in order to function properly. For the Christian community, the interplay between theology and the law results from seeking insights into what it means to be a Christian. These insights are articulated in the ecclesial community itself and articulated in the wider population of the secular domain. They are also articulated in relationship with other denominations and other religious faiths. Theology influences canon law – in fact, it is probably truer to say that theology generates canon law. Therefore, one's theological leanings will affect one's development, interpretation and administration of canon law. Maybe it is worth noting here that of the 1,752 canons in the 1983 code, most refer to the clergy in one way or another.

To be truly *of* the community the law needs to grow out of the community's understanding of itself – what it is, why it exists, what values it holds, what its purpose is in the wider community, and what it hopes for itself and the wider community as life unfolds. Communities evolve, the law needs to evolve with it or, as the canonist Ladislas Örsy SJ, in a fine essay, puts it, 'The laws will break the community or the community will break the laws' (*The Art of Interpretation*). The Christian community is meant to be shaped by the gospels before anything else. This applies as much to canon law as any other aspect of church – perhaps more so, given the potential of the law, in certain hands, to become a dry, hardened legalism that omits to give weight to the complexities of the human situation. Canon law is a means to an end – an authentic living of a Christ-centred life. If the gospel message of Jesus ceases to be the standard by which the church orders and reforms its life, that which is useful and worthy in the law will be discredited. It will be harmed by that which risks breaking the community through making an idol of the law.

Chapter Twelve

Fundamentalism

Fundamentalism is a way of thinking – it is a very particular world view that sees itself in the vanguard of safeguarding 'holy truths.' The *Modern Catholic Encyclopaedia* gives as good a definition as any: 'Fundamentalism can be broadly defined as any militant movement which seeks to protect what it sees as religious truths from the encroachment of modernity.' It does not allow for different ways of looking at the world to be valid. Even though people of a fundamentalist inclination are unlikely to see themselves as fearful, nevertheless fear is an underlying motivation. Fundamentalism fears what it sees as the corrosive effect of modern thought has on dearly held beliefs. The words 'modern' and 'liberal' are often used interchangeably by fundamentalists, and usually with disdain.

Though fundamentalism is mainly associated with religion, through religiously minded activists it can also influence politics. It might be useful to add that though it is usually associated with religion, the fundamentalist type of thinking can be applied to atheists. It can apply to those who are quite intolerant, and sometimes nasty, in their condemnation and ridicule of anything in the religious sphere. Such people brand all people of faith as being somehow deluded or ridiculous without any sense that we are not a homogenous group.

Fundamentalism is a relatively modern concept. It grew out of the Protestant tradition in the United States in the late nineteenth and early twentieth century. The name 'fundamentalism' comes from a twelve-volume work published between 1905 and 1910 called

The Fundamentals: A Testimony to the Truth. The new scientific approach to biblical criticism in the late nineteenth and early twentieth century was just one of the issues that gave rise to the publication of *The Fundamentals*. For many of the Protestant evangelical groups, the inerrancy of the Bible (every word of it is true) is an important cornerstone of belief. Though it is often identified with it, fundamentalism is not confined to Protestantism. It can be applied to the major faiths of 'The Book' – Judaism, Christianity and Islam. It is also present in Hinduism and, surprisingly, in Buddhism. Other faith systems also have their version of the fundamentalist 'option'.

Catholicism developed its own particular brand of fundamentalism during the 'modernist crisis' in the early part of the twentieth century (see Chapter Seven). Through this reaction to modernism, it managed to institutionalise fundamentalism in church structures. It created a mutation, as it were, in the church's DNA. Those Catholics of a fundamentalist leaning did not break from the church into a separate identifiable entity, but they were a distinct and motivated group. This is easily seen in the reaction to Vatican II and the sustained efforts to roll back its achievements. Fundamentalism, as defined above, remains alive and well in Catholicism, although the word tends not to be used of the mindset it describes. Catholic fundamentalism tends to be camouflaged as traditionalism, which has a less negative connotation.

The lust for certainty is one of the cornerstones of fundamentalism. The other, less obvious, underpinning is fear. Fear of the 'other', fear of the new, fear of change, fear of the unknown. This deep-rooted psychological fear, often unrecognised and therefore unacknowledged, leads to the lust for both certainty and the tribal security offered by fundamentalism. When the pace of life changes more quickly than our ability to adapt to such change, there is a sense of loss of control. Consequently, there is a strong desire to protect what it perceived important and fundamental to one's faith and life. Such a desire is easily transformed into a sense of mission.

This sense of mission can ignite an extraordinary energy and become quite a formidable force. In the practice of religion, this single-mindedness finds expression in impatience with the doubts and uncertainties that often characterise a more reflective, thoughtful faith. Though such single-mindedness has a use when it issues a challenge, it fails when it is not open to, or does not respect, an alternative point of view in response. It fails when it denies any possibility of change, resorting to clichés and slogans, when challenged by cogent argument. One such term current in Catholicism is 'à la carte Catholic'. Those who use this term with such disdain about other people fail to see that they, too, are being highly selective in picking and choosing the bits of Catholic teaching that suits their purposes. What has been shown thus far in this book is that the tradition of Catholic faith is not one simple, unchanging, linear thing. It does not take in-depth study to discover this. The most basic adult education in faith reveals it. Unfortunately, those of a fundamentalist orientation often display a remarkable resistance to education, even when they undertake formal studies.

Just as fundamentalists tend to use the words 'modern' and 'liberal' interchangeably, some people mistakenly think that fundamentalism is synonymous with conservatism. These two ways of looking at the world are not the same thing. Attempting to treat them as such is a disservice to many faith-filled, thoughtful Christians. People can be conservative without being fundamentalist. Many Catholics who would describe themselves as conservative are often thoughtful, reasonable people with a deep appreciation of the importance of education in faith. While they might be conservative in that they want to preserve what is good, precious and worthwhile, they are also open-minded and willing to be challenged. More importantly, they allow themselves to be changed by their education. This willingness to change displays particular courage because it means letting go of deeply ingrained conditioning with regard to certain beliefs. This often involves much pain and confusion. Such struggle and openness in the face of almost overwhelming challenge, is not a characteristic of fundamentalism. Having said that, conservatism is not just one identifiable homogenous group. Within conservatism the continuum runs from the moderate centre to the ultra-right-wing, which borders on, and shares much with fundamentalism, without actually becoming a fundamentalist movement. Nevertheless, it is from extreme conservatism that fundamentalism arises, from the people who think they know best for everyone else. That is its seedbed.

Just as a thinking conservatism can be a positive stance, an unthinking liberalism can be quite unhelpful in the practice of faith. An unthinking liberalism of 'anything goes' that would discard all past practices and rupture the continuum of tradition is not the antidote to fundamentalism. Quite the contrary, it only serves to confirm the fears that underpin fundamentalist thinking. It gives such thinking a credibility that it really does not deserve. Human beings, generally speaking, thrive in an orderly environment. A chaotic liberalism is no friend of a deep and reflective faith development.

One of the most attractive aspects of fundamentalism for some people is the tribal identity. Being part of a larger group offers security and identity that cannot be achieved on one's own, especially if one's sense of self is weak or non-existent. Certainty is a major foundation block of fundamentalism. It is one of its most seductive aspects for those who cannot find the security they crave in ordinary day-to-day life. We do not need a social scientist to tell us that there is a breakdown of the familial, societal and religious structures; these familiar structures formed the framework within which life was ordered and organised. The evidence is all around us. But it does not necessarily follow that society is breaking down. The old structures no longer serve our needs, therefore, we have to find new structures and the search involves trial and error. This should not be a frightening prospect – our faith in the steadfastness of the Spirit should give the faithful confidence in the process. For

some, rather unfortunately, the apparently solid structure of fundamentalism offers the promise of shelter in times of such uncertainty.
It minimises the need to move forward in faith and discernment.

A strong sense of identity is undoubtedly empowering – be it a
national identity or religious identity. One only has to look at the
loyalty given to local sports teams or political parties to understand
the powerful sense of 'belonging' to something greater than oneself.
However, when that identity is used in a hostile manner towards
those who may not agree with it, it becomes an aggressive,
overpowering force. Currently, within Catholicism, one hears more
and more emphasis on 'Catholic identity'. If this identity is about
reclaiming the centrality of the gospel message with Jesus at the
heart of things, it will be a positive development. If, however, as it
appears, it is about creating an 'us' that is separate from 'them' then
it risks falling into a fundamentalist frame of mind. A strong identity
that fosters growth is empowering. It allows an individual or group
to move forward in a life-enhancing way. A strong identity that
draws power from rigidly defined stances will always be in
opposition to the 'other'. This tribal identity will be reluctant to
engage in a conversation that might require compromise.
Ecumenism is often the casualty of a strong, fundamentalist identity.
A true and open dialogue involves vulnerability, risk and a
willingness to change. Such dialogue helps us to understand what
our central, core issues of faith are, and what is open to change.
Fundamentalism is deeply hostile towards such dialogue and to the
ecumenical spirit. It sees openness to others as a weakness and a
betrayal of the truth.

If a group can claim that it is the faithful keeper of the truth, it
really does not need any further legitimisation. It does not need the
nuanced interpretation of the sacred word by scripture scholars and
theologians who may be perceived as diluting the word of God.
Fundamentalism looks at the world and the church and sees signs
of decay and moral disintegration. The only way it can deal with this

is a reaffirmation of what are seen as 'fundamental truths'. This reaffirmation becomes a battle – the faithful remnant (a biblical concept from the Hebrew scriptures) fights for the faith. This is a very seductive image indeed. Fundamentalism can be quite militant in its expression. The 'protection' of the truth is seen as a battle against modern influence. For Catholic fundamentalists, orthodoxy is paramount. It is worth pausing here for a moment to consider the word orthodoxy. It is sometimes used (wrongly) in a disparaging way to describe rigid adherence to rules. But this is to do it an injustice. The word comes from the Greek (hardly surprising!) and means 'right belief'. There is a related word, *orthopraxis*, which means 'right practice'. For most reflective Catholics orthodoxy feeds into orthopraxis, and orthopraxis informs orthodoxy. It is truer to speak of a 'narrow orthodoxy' when describing something rigid and inflexible about faith or church practice. For fundamentalists, adhering to declared doctrine is everything. Unfortunately, they interpret doctrine in a very narrow sense. For them the church simply cannot change – its doctrine is clear for everyone to see.

In fundamentalism of all stripes, the eternal truths of faith are seen as something outside the person. They are understood to have an independent existence that stands apart from and is not affected by history and culture. This is seen in the inerrancy of the Bible in Protestant fundamentalist groups. For Catholic fundamentalism it is seen in the 'unchanging church' and especially in the rite of the Tridentine Latin liturgy. Change in the celebration of the liturgy was agreed by the bishops of the Second Vatican Council, after the first set of debates on the subject. The vote was: 1,992 in favour, 11 against, with a further 180 in favour when certain agreed changes were made. This was anathema to small groups of people in various countries who could not understand or accept the change. While some conservative groups had great difficulty with the change, nevertheless they accepted it as part of the church's engagement with the modern world.

Fundamentalists refused to accept the change. They formed groups, which could not in the strict sense be called 'breakaway groups'. Nevertheless, they refused to accept the changes of Vatican II. Usually these groups were led by priests who organised Latin masses for the dissenters from Vatican II. There were many different groups who repudiated the Second Vatican Council, but they did not make common cause with each other. Each had its own specific core issue to defend. Some of the language used by these groups, and which continues to characterise fundamentalist groups, can be quite intolerant. They have accused the church leadership of 'conspiring with the enemies of the church' and 'acting as the fifth-column of Satan'; they believe there are conspiracies within the church whose only intention is to destroy the church from within. There is even a group who will not recognise any pope after Pius XII. Its members assert that all recent popes were not legitimate popes, and that the seat of Peter is vacant.

Another change with which Catholic fundamentalists could not cope was the levelling out of the distinction between the priestly caste and the rest of the church. Vatican II moved the church from the hierarchical model to a more (or less) egalitarian sense of church as the People of God. In the pre-Vatican II church, clerics had an enhanced status from an understanding that they had 'special knowledge' about revelation and matters sacred. This in turn fostered a deferential attitude in the lay members of church. It was part of popular catechetical teaching that in honouring the priest, people were 'showing honour and reverence to Christ Himself, for the priest is in a very true sense, another Christ' (*Fundamentalisms Observed*, p. 93). Many traditionalists in the church could not cope with this blurring of distinction. It is interesting to note that many of the conservative groups formed because of difficulties with this concept, arose from lay initiatives. Those seeking a more modern church find much to draw upon from Vatican II. Because of the compromise in many of the Vatican documents, those who need to hold to previous concepts find much there also. This allows all shades of opinion to find some comfort.

In the more fundamentalists groups, however, almost all of the revolts were led by clerics. In these groups the clergy maintained the key positions of power and authority and all the rituals are very much clerically centred. One of these groups was eventually excommunicated by Pope John Paul II in 1988. This was led by Archbishop Lefèbvre, a French bishop who had been one of the bishops at the Council. He was horrified at the changes he saw happening as a result of the Council, especially the changes in the liturgy. Lefèbvre formed the group the Society of Pius X, named for the pope of the anti-modernist campaign. Apart from keeping the Latin Mass, groups such as Lefèbvre's also place great emphasis on the separateness of the priestly caste. At an ordination of priests for his Society in 1976, Lefèbvre said:

> By this idea of power bestowed on the lower rank on the Holy Mass, they [liturgical reformers] have destroyed the priesthood! They are destroying the priesthood, for what is the priest, if the priest no longer has a personal power, the power given to him by his ordination, as these future priests are going to receive in a moment? They are going to receive a character, a character that will put them above the people of God! Never more … shall they be able to say 'We are men like other men.' This would not be true. They will no longer be men like other men! They will be men of God. They will be men, I should say, who almost participate in the divinity of Our Lord Jesus Christ by His sacerdotal [meaning 'priestly'] character.
>
> Quoted in *Fundamentalisms Observed*

Though it excommunicated him, the Vatican has made significant efforts over the years to reconnect with Lefèbvre's schismatic community. Lefèbvre rebuffed all overtures, yet the attitude towards him and his movement remained the focus of efforts towards reconciliation. This continued with Benedict XVI, who conceded most of what Lefèbvre demanded, despite which, the dissident bishop reneged on his agreement to resume communion with Rome. The attitude towards this group seems extraordinarily tolerant and benevolent. Particularly so when one considers how other members of the church who have not broken away, but try to look for reform from within, have been treated. Such people have been silenced and threatened with expulsion for attempting to keep the church alive in a society that is becoming increasingly secular and within which the church is becoming marginalised.

It ought to have become obvious from all the previous chapters that much of theology and faith practice is more of a 'both/and' rather than an 'either/or' concept. The 'both/and' model allows for scope and imagination in thinking. The 'either/or' tends to see in black and white. This distinction in understanding is of supreme importance in the political sphere. When people of a fundamentalist orientation latch onto socio-political issues, as they do, unfortunately, they 'see too clearly to see well'. They bring their black and white thinking to issues that have many layers to their understanding. They often stir up and play upon people's fear on a variety of issues – very often regarding the family *vis-à-vis* the State. Issues like divorce, availability of birth control, and of course, abortion, not to mention civil rights for gay, lesbian, bisexual and transgendered people, are a fertile ground for fundamentalist and ultraconservative passions. Freedom of speech is a vital democratic right. Responsible use of that freedom ought to be a natural response to the privilege of that right. Fundamentalists tend not to accord that freedom of speech quite the respect it deserves. Their propensity to incite fear as opposed to making their case by reasoned argument does not serve democracy well. In inciting fear, they do not always respect the importance of presenting factual information to support their cause. Having said that, there is also the responsibility of the greater population not to allow itself to be bent to the will of a small group through unfounded fear. There is the responsibility to search out the facts of whatever the issue happens to be. This is not difficult to do now, with so much information at our fingertips. As Gabriel Daly concluded in a paper to the Glenstal Ecumenical Conference (*Catholic Fundamentalism*) on Catholic Fundamentalism many years ago, 'The Gospel faces us with the difficult task of loving them – while standing up to them.'

CHAPTER THIRTEEN

Translation of the Missal

In 2011 the new English translation of the missal was imposed by the Vatican on the English-speaking world. The intention of this translation is to make the English text of the Mass a more direct literal translation of the Latin. This action caused much anger in the various countries where it happened, with good reason. It has put faithfulness to a particular language above the participation of the gathered community. Latin is an interesting language certainly, but it is a dead language.

Historically, many people held a mistaken belief that Latin is a sacred language. It is not. Latin was the administrative language of the Roman empire, particularly the western part of the empire. The original language of Christian worship and scriptures was Greek. This was a cultural and administrative relic of the ancient Greek empire that had once ruled the area. There was also a certain amount of bilingualism, where the formal language of empire was used alongside the local language. Just like Latin, ancient Greek was not a sacred language either. It was the language of the educated classes in the Near and Middle East two thousand years ago. Where Christianity spread beyond these areas of Greek influence, the language of worship was the local mother tongue. So, even from the beginning, there were as many as seven different languages of worship. As the Christian liturgy developed and moved from an oral form to a written text, Greek was the language most commonly used for the written material. It was only in the third century CE, because of political issues, that Latin began to take over from Greek as the language of public worship in the western part of the Roman empire. It is interesting to note that in Rome itself, it took another century or so to move from Greek to Latin, because of the more conservative nature of Christian worship here.

Having a single language in the various provinces of the Roman empire was useful for civil and military administration, and for commerce and culture. It can be compared to the use of English in international finance or aviation today. English is now the designated official international language of aviation. It is not enough to have the limited knowledge of specialised phrases directly connected to flying. Air traffic controllers and flight crew members engaged in international flights need to be proficient in English. It makes sense. It gets the job done efficiently and reduces the chance of error in understanding instructions. Latin in church fulfilled a similar function. It became the language of ecclesiastical empire – useful, practical, but not sacred.

Language is an important part of identity. It is through language, written and oral, that we articulate meaning about the external world around us and the internal world of thoughts and emotions. We also articulate meaning through ritual by means of gestures and symbols. However, as vehicles for meaning, the written and spoken language predominates. It is how we tell our story. Therefore, words are important.

The gathering of people for Mass is the community of Christians coming together and articulating their faith in God in a public way. We need to tell our story – first to ourselves, and then to others. We come together because of the example of Jesus Christ drawing people to himself in communities and groups, from all walks of life. This is not the action of empires or large corporations for whom people as a whole are merely numbers. This is the action of small communities where people are known by name – where people matter. The language of empire is not the language of community.

Faith is expressed in particular geographical places in particular times in history, by people with a particular set of life experiences. These experiences are drawn from the traditions, both good and bad, that have formed them. Language and modes of expression reflect this experience. That is why using the language of empire is not suitable for worship. Certainly, having stable texts that transmit the faith experience through a recognisable liturgy allows each generation to connect with the tradition. But this connection must be forged in its own way, as a living, breathing tradition, not as an acceptance of a fossilised text that is immune to new interpretation. We only need to look at ourselves and how our attitudes and opinions are moulded, changed and refined through our experiences. Language also needs to be able to reflect this movement. One of the most obvious ways to reflect movement in thought and understanding is the use of inclusive language in the liturgy.

Unfortunately, the new translation now in use since 2011 is an attempt to fossilise the liturgy. Its purpose is to make the English text as close to a literal translation of the Latin as possible. Part of this adherence to Latin is the disappearance of inclusive language. Man and Men are now the standard expression of both male and female. Another problem is the use of exalted language from a bygone era grafted onto a modern text. It resulted in stilted and awkward phrases that grate on the ear and are out of place in community worship. What is difficult to understand is that this translation runs contrary to many developments in the post-Vatican II church. Best practice in translation is to communicate the ideas and thoughts expressed in the original language as accurately as possible into the translated language. Literal, word for word translation usually has the effect of poorly representing thoughts and ideas.

A special papal commission was set up by Paul VI to oversee the proper implementation of the new *Constitution on the Liturgy* approved at Vatican II. This commission drew up an excellent document on the translation of liturgical documents in January 1969. This was given a French title: *Comme le Prevoit* (*As Forseen*). The principles of this document are as valid today as they were forty-four years ago – a testament to the skill and knowledge of those who drew it up. It says:

> The purpose of liturgical translations is to proclaim the message of salvation to believers and to express the prayer of the Church to the Lord ... To achieve this end, it is not sufficient that a liturgical translation merely reproduce the expressions and ideas of the original text. Rather it must faithfully communicate to a given people, and in their own language, that which the Church by means of this given text originally intended to communicate to another people in another time. A faithful translation, therefore, cannot be judged on the basis of individual words: the total context of this specific act of communication must be kept in mind, as well as the literary form proper to the respective language.
>
> Thus, in the case of liturgical communication, it is necessary to take into account not only the message to be conveyed, but also the speaker, the audience, and the style. Translations, therefore, must be faithful to the art of communication in all its various aspects, but especially in regard to the message itself, in regard to the audience for which it is intended, and in regard to the manner of expression.
>
> *Comme le Prevoit*, §6 & §7

In the opening paragraph of *Comme le Prevoit*, the special commission recognised that any translation undertaken would need to be reviewed after experiment and the passage of time. They never expected to see a perfect translation first time around. All of the relevant post-conciliar documents in the immediate aftermath of Vatican II, taken together with the *Constitution on the Liturgy*, leave very little doubt as to what was intended by the Council Fathers with regard to translation.

A person deeply involved with the work of translation was Fr John Fitzsimmons. The late Fr Fitzsimmons was a biblical scholar.

For fifteen years, he was chairman of the advisory committee of the International Commission on English in the Liturgy (ICEL). For ten of those years he was a consultor to the Vatican's Congregation for Divine Worship (CDW).

In a letter about the translation to the Catholic paper *The Tablet*, Fr Fitzsimmons wrote: 'One can only assume that this nonsense will be inflicted on us as long as the shepherds of the local Churches put up with it' (26 May 2001). He was responding to the publication of *Liturgiam Authenticam* (*Authentic Liturgy*), an ill-advised, ill-informed Vatican document on the liturgy. It was, in effect, the blueprint for the current translation of the Roman missal. Fr Fitzsimmons saw this document as

> the last in long line of ill-informed, heavy-handed and negative measures adopted by the Congregation for Divine Worship ... [which] is part of a much wider agenda which seeks to centralise everything in Rome, even things that Rome has proved ... incompetent to handle.

Given his credentials, he spoke with an authority that cannot be ignored. But it is not just an issue of language, important though that is. It runs much deeper than that. It is about control and abuse of power. This translation is contrary to a number of important principles. It is contrary to the spirit and reality of Vatican II's *Constitution on the Liturgy*. It is contrary to the norms of justice in how ICEL was subverted. It is contrary to the spirit of ecumenism. It is contrary to a very important part of Catholic social teaching – the principle of subsidiarity. It is contrary to sound academic principles and, finally, it is contrary to canon law (Given the adversarial nature of law, some would dispute the issue of canon law, however, I stand by my claim).

Given the limitations of space, and the purpose of this book, I will take a brief look at just two of these issues – the subversion of ICEL and ecumenism (I deal with all six issues in an article published in *Doctrine & Life*, vol. 61, no. 4, 2011).

ICEL was a legitimately constituted body set up in 1963 by the main episcopal conferences in the English-speaking world, including Ireland. A significant number of other conferences, in countries where multiple dialects existed, decided that the English translation would be beneficial for their pastoral purposes also. They became associate members of the commission. ICEL had teams of experts in various disciplines relevant to the task. Its mandate was to work out a plan for the translation of liturgical texts and the provision of original texts, where required, in language which would be correct, dignified, intelligible and suitable for recitation and singing.

ICEL, as a commission on the liturgy, did its job well, but never claimed the first translations of the early 1970s were perfect – just as *Comme le Prevoit* had anticipated. They were translated faithfully, under the acceptable norms of translation, and in keeping with the Vatican II document *Constitution on the Liturgy*. Unfortunately, the pressure of time to get the texts 'out there' meant that some phrasing lacked a beauty desirable in liturgical texts. By 1982 the revision of the missal had begun. Fifteen years of dedicated work went into the revised translations, during which time relations with the Vatican's Congregation for Divine Worship (CDW) were mostly cordial and effective. That is, until 1998 when the Chilean Cardinal Jorge Medina Estévez was brought to Rome and put in charge of the CDW. A systematic takeover was set in train, such that if it were to happen in the political sphere, it would be considered akin to a *coup d'état*.

Unsubstantiated allegations were made against the executive secretary of ICEL, Dr John Page. Dr Page is a layman dedicated to his church, who had given twenty years of loyal service to ICEL. In a letter to the then chairman of the Episcopal Board, Bishop Maurice Taylor, in October 1999, Cardinal Medina accused Dr Page of taking 'certain liberties'. These unsubstantiated allegations were never specified, and were seen as false by those who worked with Dr Page. Fearing his continued presence would damage ICEL, Dr Page felt he had no option but to resign. ICEL was then ordered by CDW to incorporate, among others, the following in their constitution:

- ICEL was forbidden to provide any more original texts to and was ordered to cease having contacts with 'bodies pertaining to non-Catholic ecclesial communities'.

- 'Careful reconfiguration' of the main office of the executive secretary was to take place.

- ICEL employees were to be on fixed-term contracts, with any extensions being reserved to the Congregation for Divine Worship.

- Everyone working for ICEL (except episcopal board members) had to receive clearance from the congregation;

- The redrafting of ICEL's statutes was to be done directly and exclusively by the bishops of ICEL.

The revised translations that were fifteen years in the making, because of the care given to them, were rejected out of hand. The CDW implied that many bishops were unhappy with the translations. This was a very strange claim since ICEL was a bishops' commission. There was ample opportunity for any bishop, who so desired, to voice his concerns at any point during the preparations.

As people finished their terms of office and retired, ICEL more and more became an extension of the Vatican's Congregation for Divine Worship. In 2009 a Fr Andrew Wadsworth, well-known celebrant of the Tridentine Rite (Latin Mass), was appointed as the executive secretary, the post formerly held by Dr Page. Then, rather strangely, a specially formed committee, called *Vox Clara* (*Clear Voice*) was set up by the Congregation for Divine Worship. This committee did not have a clearly defined role, nor was there transparency in the selection of its members. Yet it was set up as an extra layer of oversight on the diminished ICEL.

This brief summary only skims the surface of the ICEL story which is worth reading in depth – even if it is heartbreaking in its conclusion. Bishop Maurice Taylor's slim book, *It's the Eucharist, Thank God*, published by Decani Books contains the full story, told by a man who witnessed it. What is telling, though, is the speed with which the Congregation for Divine Worship, as an arm of the Vatican's administration, could react to ICEL and dismantle its collegial structure. It stands in stark contrast to the lethargy of the Vatican's response to clerical child sexual abuse and its systematic cover-up.

One of the benefits of liturgical renewal in church was the increased cooperation with other Christians. ICEL played a critical role in this ecumenical contact. National and international ecumenical groups took the lead from ICEL and formed English-language consultation groups on liturgy. A number of agreed common texts for prayers developed and were appreciated by all concerned. Catholic renewal had a significant impact on Protestant worship. So much so that an ecumenical version of the Roman lectionary was produced. The ecumenical opportunities at this time were without parallel. Horace T. Allen, a Calvinist Presbyterian, states that 'the Lectionary and the use of the Christian calendar have transformed Protestant worship in the English-speaking world'. A singular benefit of this was the joy it brought to Christian couples who belonged to different ecclesial communities (more crudely known as 'mixed marriages'), who were able to share the same Word in both liturgies.

Horace Allen, as co-chairman of the steering committee of the international ecumenical group on English language liturgy, visited Rome in 1994 to request that the Congregation for Divine Worship allow for some experimental use by Catholics of the Lectionary system that ecumenical Protestants had produced

> to bring Christians of all languages and continents into *audible* unity around the table of the Word of God … We long for the continued official participation of the Holy See in the most universal *and* local experience of unity.
>
> *Liturgical Renewal as a Way to Christian Unity*

Mr Allen's request was ignored and he received no response.

What an opportunity lost! Just imagine the joy of a true ecumenical encounter; not the superficial ecumenism over smiles and cups of tea, but the real ecumenism in sharing the Word. This vision of ecumenism was lost on Cardinal George Pell, Chairman of *Vox Clara*. He was reported as saying that it is more important to have a new Catholic translation of the Mass than to have common texts for prayers that English-speaking Christians can use together (*The Tablet*, 20 November 2004, p. 33). Perhaps Mr Allen, can express it better:

And as I read this document [*Liturgiam Authenticam*], I realised that something terrible had happened that in my worst imagining I had never anticipated. That a trusted ecumenical partner would walk away from the table. And, in fact, walk away so deliberately as to dismiss the others at the table, such as 'mixed commissions who do not represent their communions' or who represent their 'communions of insignificant numbers.' I never knew that in the Christian church you needed more than two or three. But that's what it says. ... I went to the sacred Basilica of St Peter, knelt down and prayed before the body of Pope John XXIII. And I thought ... how strange: *his body is in glory and his Council is in ruins* [emphasis in original].

Tradition is the byword of those who favour the Latin Mass rite. Traditionalists tend not to appreciate the benefits of an inculturated liturgy. But tradition is not the same as imitation, and likewise, inculturation is not the same as novelty. As Peter Jeffrey, a chant historian, says, they are

two sides of the same coin ... for tradition is the record of inculturations past, a storehouse of models and resources for inculturations of today, which in turn will generate the traditions of the future.

Jeffrey, *Translating Tradition*

Unfortunately such an appreciation of tradition and culture did not exist in the Congregation for Divine Worship from 1998 to 2002. Instead we have had a ham-fisted attempt at some kind of part-Tridentine restoration which cannot but fail. Such a restoration is not possible, but that is not good news, because what we are likely to get instead, according to Peter Jeffery, is a

> crude caricature of it, vastly more impoverished and repressive than the original ever was. There are none-too-subtle indications that this is just what *LA's* [*Liturgiam Authenticam*] talk of a new era really means.

In 1972, eight members of the International Theological Commission wrote to Pope Paul VI to voice their concern that the 'unity and purity' of the Catholic faith was being undermined by the translations from the Latin to the vernacular. Two prominent members of this group were Josef Ratzinger and, the Chilean, Jorge Medina Estévez, who later became cardinal.

It's worth stepping back in time slightly to make a useful comparison. In 1966, the ink was barely dry on the almost unanimous report of the Pontifical Commission for the Study of Population, Family and Births made to Pope Paul VI when a small group of four clerics set about its reversal (see Chapter Nine). A very small group managed to 'reconvert' the pope to the *status quo ante*. The seismic impact on the church of this subversion of the thoughtful, reasoned process of the Commission is still being felt. Perhaps then, it is no surprise that the current translation mess would appear to have its origins in the revolt of a small group swimming against the tide of history and experience.

This is why the current Roman Missal issue is greater than the issue of translation. It is the forced acceptance of a particular vision of church. It represents an ecclesiology (the study of church) that is exclusive and narrow; an ecclesiology that has little time for collegial governance. There is little appreciation for academic freedom where peer review acts as natural checks and balances. It displays a patronising attitude, if not outright disdain, towards ecumenism and is functionally misogynistic. It operates out of an institutional model of liturgy that favours hierarchism and clericalism (It is worth noting here that in his letter to the people of Ireland, Pope Benedict XVI quotes John Vianney to express his vision of priesthood: 'The priest holds the key to the treasures of heaven: it is he who opens the door: he is the steward of the good Lord; the administrator of his goods'). It creates a pyramidal, law-centred model of church where observance of the rules and regulations are paramount. Liturgy becomes a legalistic consideration and the lay faithful are primarily passive. It is an ecclesiology that is, in effect, subverting the organic development of the reforms of the Second Vatican Council. Reforms that received the vote of the great majority of bishops present.

The bishops of Vatican II took some time to find their collective voice, but when they did so, mountains moved. The bishops of the present day have a responsibility to carry on the reform that began in such good faith. The Irish bishops had an excellent opportunity to serve not only the Irish faithful, but English-speaking Catholics worldwide, if they could have found the courage to reject the imposed translation. Unfortunately, it was yet another opportunity lost.

At a liturgy of lament and repentance in Dublin (20 February 2011), Archbishop Diarmuid Martin said that 'there is still a long path to journey in honesty' before the clerical church can truly merit forgiveness over the sexual abuse scandals. Witnessing the naked abuse of power which has lead to the ill-planned, ill-informed translation, it is not unreasonable to claim that 'there is still a long path to journey in honesty'. A journey in honesty to where the clerical church will finally accept the endemic nature of the abuse of power at the core of its administration.

Colluding with the abuse of power is always wrong. Perhaps it is fitting to leave the final words to Bishop Maurice Taylor, the last chairman of the original ICEL:

[I]t is tantalising to wonder how the Congregation [CDW], or indeed the Holy See itself, would have reacted if the conferences of bishops, or even the conference presidents, had claimed their legitimate authority had been infringed by the congregation's behaviour. Such a complaint was, I think, not put forward strongly enough. If it had been, is it too fanciful to dream that it might have led to a thorough examination of the role and activities of the Roman Curia?

Taylor, It's the Eucharist, Thank God

CHAPTER FOURTEEN

Priesthood

As with much else in church, the development of a clerical priesthood took time to evolve. This is neither strange nor surprising. The central focus of the Christian celebration – the Eucharist – also evolved and changed over time. It changed from a simple household meal to a large gathering in a building specially designed for that purpose. The early Eucharist was very much about remembrance of Jesus and his actions. The prayers were simple and short and in everyday language. They focused mainly on thanksgiving (the word Eucharist comes from the Greek, and means thanksgiving). There is no mention of consecration in the early Eucharist. By the fourth century CE, Christianity was an official religion within the Roman Empire. It was in competition with many other forms of worship of multiple gods since its inception. It is unfortunate, but not altogether surprising, that it took on the trappings of other contemporary religions when it became a tolerated religion. This included having temples, altars, a distinct priesthood (as opposed to the priesthood of all the people, which had existed in the fledgling church of the first century) and other features of religious worship. The domestic meal became a symbolic ritual where most of those present no longer actively participated. The prayers had become longer and expressed in more exalted language. The worshipping group ceased to be participants and had become viewers who watched, at a remove, the 'specialist' performing the ritual.

The householders, men and women who presided over the Eucharist, no longer had a place. The priestly caste evolved and became the 'professionals' of the church. The focus of Eucharist as thanksgiving shifted over time to that of sacrifice and of consecration. The variety of rituals in various geographical locations began to lose their local flavour and become part of a more uniform expression. There is nothing extraordinary in all of this. Rituals tend to move from the simple to the complex as time passes. The question needs to be asked: why is it, in this evolution of the Eucharist, that women were pushed to the margins and beyond? Why were they, who figured significantly in the public life of Jesus, deemed, by their very being, unsuitable to lead the community in worship in his name?

Historically and in many cultures, the exclusion of women from wider participation in society has been based on the belief that they were inferior beings. This attitude towards women helped to limit their access to education and their leadership roles outside the immediate family. In the life of the early church there were a few decades where women had the opportunity to fulfil their role in church as evangelists spreading the Good News of the Risen Christ. But as the patriarchal influence of the surrounding culture reasserted itself, this was extinguished by the second century CE. One of the main influences on the view of women within the Christian community was the biblical story of Eve. Eve was seen as the person who let evil into the world by her disobedience. This idea was based on a literal interpretation of the bible, with very destructive results for women in the church. Early church writings on women have a strong association with Eve, and are perceived in a very negative light. The significant influence of Greek philosophy in Catholicism has also contributed greatly to the perception of women as lesser human beings. In Aristotle's philosophy, which was hugely influential in the church from the middle-ages, a woman is considered a 'misbegotten' male.

The occasional exception to the general exclusion of women would be that of the ruling classes. Their wealth gave them power and, sometimes, the chance of education. Of course, through the church's history, there were still the occasional women of independent means, often widows, who had the opportunity to use their independence to broaden their horizons. There were also single women who pushed the established boundaries in their social activism. The clerical leaders of the church had quite a problem with these independent women with strong social consciences. They eventually managed to corral them into groups that became congregations of religious sisters, who were ultimately controlled by the male power-holders in the church. One such person was Mary Ward who set up a group of women, free from male rule, to work with the poor. It is hardly surprising that eventually, but not in her own lifetime, her group of workers were forced to accept being bounded by the convent. Her story is well worth reading on two counts. Firstly, because of the courage of the woman herself, given that she lived and ministered in the late sixteenth and early seventeenth centuries. Secondly, because four centuries later, the attitude of the Vatican to women stills remains deeply hostile.

Feminist theology was an important development in the church following Vatican II. This was not a new development, though. There were women who attempted to claim their place in other Christian denominations, with considerable success, from the nineteenth century forward. The difference within Catholicism is that feminist theology coincided with the general feminist movement that occurred in the 1960s and 1970s in the US and Europe, when women in these places began to find their voices. They challenged the idea that the norm and standard for humanity as a whole was the male of the species. As women found their voices in the secular world, it is hardly surprising that those with vocations to priesthood began to find theirs within Catholicism. As early as 1967 a book entitled *The Question of Women and the Priesthood* was published. This was a careful examination of the issue by Sr Vincent Emmanuel Hannon, an Irish sister of La Sainte Union congregation. She concluded:

> [i]t can be stated with confidence that the question of a female priesthood is open to free discussion and calls for further investigation before it can be declared as having been decided once and for all by divine law. The final word must rest with the magisterium of the Church, which is the pillar and the ground of truth. She alone with confidence can ask the question: 'Is the participation of women in the priesthood possible under the Christian dispensation?' for she alone as the Bride of Christ has within the depths of her own life the answer, which can be formulated and finally expressed only when serious reflection has been given to the question.
>
> Hannon, *The Question of Women and the Priesthood*

Sr Hannon's work shows the deference common at the time to church hierarchy in her final paragraph, which might grate on twenty-first-century ears. Yet she clearly states that the answer to women's ordination can 'be formulated and finally expressed only when serious reflection has been given to the question'.

Part of the serious reflection needed depends on how we frame the question of women in church. Historically, discussion of women's participation in church was coloured by the existing bias against them. Where there was mention of women, the arguments put forward already had as their starting point that women were inferior beings. So the outcome of the argument or discussions could never be in doubt. The answer was already built into the question.

When the issue of women's ordination arose in the post-Vatican II years, there was a welcome change in how the question was framed and in the process of reflecting on it. On Paul VI's instruction, the Pontifical Biblical Commission was asked to study the evidence from scripture that might answer the question posed to it: 'Whether or not women can be ordained to priestly ministry (especially as ministers of the eucharist and as leaders of the Christian community).'

154

This commission composed of priests – no women and no lay biblical scholars – applied itself to the task. After a forensic examination, the evidence from scripture could not answer the question one way or the other. So, there was no scriptural barrier to women's ordination. If, as Sr Hannon suggested, serious reflection was applied to the results of the Commission's deliberations, those who control the power in the church might have learned that women, as well as men, are called to priesthood. Unfortunately, the immediate response was to bury the 1976 report of the Commission, and reaffirm the reasons why women cannot be ordained. These are:

1. The example of scripture of Christ only choosing his apostles from among men.

2. The constant practice of the church which has imitated Christ in only choosing men.

3. The living, teaching authority of the church which has 'consistently held that the exclusion of women from the priesthood is in common with God's plan for his church'.

These arguments are very weak indeed. The first reason fails as a result of the Pontifical Biblical Commission's own study – scripture does not prohibit women's ordination. The second reason does not hold up because it is generally accepted by scripture scholars that the twelve apostles symbolically represent the twelve tribes of Israel. Jesus was a Jew who was bringing a message to the Jewish people at large – the twelve represented this totality. The third fails because an examination of dogma and doctrine shows that 'consistent' teaching is much less consistent than is believed. Also, it is very important to realise that Jesus did not ordain anybody, not the Twelve, nor anybody else. Jesus had women as well as men among his closest disciples. It is worth remembering that in the gospels, the news of the resurrection was given to women first. Yet this is an event in scripture that is very much played down. One cannot help but think if Simon Peter was the first to the tomb, the significance would not be underplayed in the same way.

155

As mentioned above, the response of the Biblical Commission was not to the liking of those who commissioned it and the report was not made public. Only for the fact that a French version of it was leaked to the press, the results would never have been known. It is interesting to note that in the list of Pontifical Biblical Commission reports listed on the Vatican website, this report from 1976 is omitted. The list of documents starts at 1905 and runs to 2008. There are thirty-six documents in all, but the document from 1976 is not listed. The dates jump from 1974 to 1984 with nothing for 1976!

Following the suppression of the Biblical Commission's report, the Congregation for the Doctrine of the Faith issued a document called *Inter Insigniores*. This reaffirmed the three 'arguments' above against women's ordination. Perhaps the CDF assumed that this document would be the last word on the issue. But that was not the case. The issue kept returning for discussion among various groups and was gathering momentum.

It is interesting to note here that the writer(s) of *Inter Insigniores* quote St Thomas Aquinas as part of their argument that women did not represent the maleness of Christ, which was a major stumbling block to ordination. When scholars examined the CDF's document it was discovered that St Thomas was misrepresented. The citation gave the impression that maleness was intrinsic to priesthood. Given the monumental importance of St Thomas in the church's tradition, this was seen as a powerful argument. However, when a scripture scholar, John R. Donahue examined the text, he discovered the citation was broken off mid-sentence, but was presented as being complete. When the quotation was checked, it was discovered that the reason Thomas Aquinas argued against women's ordination was because 'a woman is in the state of subjection, she cannot receive the sacrament of orders'. Women's perceived inferiority, not the maleness of Christ, was Thomas's argument. One of the central pillars of the CDF's argument fails as a result of its own scholarly dishonesty.

Despite all efforts to halt them, the discussions on women's ordination continued to grow. Before they could reach critical mass, however, they were brought to an abrupt halt in 1994. This was when John Paul II issued a document called *Ordinatio Sacerdotalis* (*Priestly Ordination*), unilaterally declaring that there *was* a scriptural basis for women's exclusion. This was declared despite the Biblical Commission's report which found no exclusion and despite the fact he was not a biblical scholar. Not only that, but he declared that exclusion of women from orders was to be *definitively held*. This is the very disturbing term that is used to give a document the cloak of 'infallibility' even though it does not fulfil the criteria for such a declaration (see Chapter Six). Coincidentally, in 1994 Sr Lavinia Byrne wrote a book, *Woman at the Altar: The Ordination of Women in the Catholic Church*. This book was going through the printers when the document was issued by John Paul II forbidding, once and for all, ordination for women. Even though it was awkward for her publishers, Sr Lavinia insisted that the pope's apostolic letter be included in her book as an appendix. *Woman at the altar* was reprinted in 1998 and again 1999. It was eventually suppressed by the Vatican. There was speculation that remaining stocks of the book were pulped by the publishers – the modern equivalent of a book burning, but this was never officially confirmed (There are still plenty of second-hand copies of *Woman at the Altar* on-line). Eventually Sr Lavinia Byrne left her congregation in order to protect its leaders from the bullying tactics of the Vatican who were putting severe pressure on them to limit her activities.

Even though the actions of the Vatican as mentioned above were focused on women's ordination, there is a wider issue of women's voices being heard. Ordination is only one part of that story. In the 1980s the US bishops took an interesting initiative based on the insight of Vatican II that the church is all the People of God. They prepared two important pastoral documents, one on war and peace and one on the economy. As part of the preparation of these documents, they engaged in extensive listening sessions with people expert in the relevant fields. The resulting pastoral letters were received with great interest and respect by people outside as well as inside church. Given the effectiveness of this process, when the bishops began the process of preparing a document on women, they engaged in the same process of wide consultation. However, midway through this listening and discerning process the US bishops were notified by the Vatican that their method of research and consultation was unacceptable and it had to be abandoned. They did not use this broad listening process in any subsequent documents.

The issue of women's ordination is not a women's rights issue, but it is most definitely about how women are valued. Yet, it is greater than just women alone. It is about church and community and leadership within that community. It is about the message of Jesus Christ coming alive in the community – not just at Eucharist, but as something that sustains people's hope and influences their actions. Communities do not need people who perform a type of magical action with bread and wine to make Jesus present. Jesus is truly present in the community as it gathers in prayer and thanksgiving – this was the belief of the early church. Real Presence existed long before the concept of consecration developed and long, long before the development of transubstantiation, which is a twelfth-century philosophical concept. Communities need gatherers and leaders to bring people together and to give structure to how belief is expressed through ritual. One does not need to be male nor celibate to be a gatherer or a leader – men and women, married and single have the capacity to build community.

Many communities of Catholics around the world are deprived of the Eucharistic celebration simply because there are not enough celibate men to perform the function. This is nothing short of scandalous. The thinking behind it (I hesitate to call it the theology behind it) is that Christ is male, therefore priest have to be male. (Why decide on maleness as the norm? Why not ethnicity? Jesus was a Jew, through and through – it was as a Jew that he preached. Why not stipulate that only Palestinian Christians can be priests? It makes just as much sense.)

As the saying goes, the victors write the history. Those who control the information control what is said, how it is said and how much is said. Those in power in the Vatican are convinced that women have no place in ministerial priesthood and that this is God's plan. If this is true, then it should not be necessary to hide reports, interfere with consultative processes, and to insist that the matter is closed and should not be discussed. If is not of God, it will fail without any assistance from human beings. But if it is of God, then maybe it is the Spirit who causes the question to return despite all attempts at suppression. Perhaps, it might be enlightening to view the issue of women's ordination more as an issue of the anti-modernism that still lives and breathes in the church. In his book *Ordaining Women*, Mark Chaves argues 'that the Church's resistance to full gender equality, and its expression of that resistance in terms of its core sacramentalist identity, should also be understood in the context of constructing a boundary between the Church and the world' (p. 124). Because the church has been forced to give up so much in terms of its power and influence in the past century, it is still trying to prove that there is space between it and the world at large.

Just as the Eucharist evolved in its ritual celebration, the notion of priesthood has evolved. It has gone from being in the place of Christ at the table of Eucharist, to being in the image of Christ. Needless to say, this exalted image developed from within the priestly caste itself. Priests have become central to the ritual in a way that is depriving people of what should be the most natural thing for Christians to do – gather in joy and hope, sorrow and repentance, to praise and give thanks for the great gift of God to humankind: the incarnation of God's love in Jesus, the Risen Christ. Women as well as men, both married and single, can do this.

Chapter Fifteen

Sexual Abuse in Church

The child sexual abuse scandal in the church is a sordid, horrible story that highlights all that is worst in church and taints all that is good. But much worse than that, sexual abuse destroys lives. It has also been described by some survivors of abuse as murder of the soul. It is destructive, it is sordid and it is horrible, but it is not new. For as long as the church has existed there has been need to speak against it. There is a church document from the latter half of the first century CE called *The Didache* (also known as *The Teaching of the Twelve Apostles*). This is a series of instructions set out for the early Christians about behaviour and worship and also instructions for those preparing for baptism. Instruction 2:2 states among other things 'do not murder; do not commit adultery; do not practice pederasty [sexual activity with minors]'. In the early fourth century there is a canon from a local council or synod held in Elvira in Spain which, among other harsh punishments for sexual sins in general committed by clergy in relation to women, specifically mentions that 'men who sexually abuse boys shall not be given communion at the end'. Though this canon does not single out clergy, it is clear that the issue of sexual abuse was not something to be tolerated.

One particular monk, Peter Damian, wrote a scathing treatise around 1050 CE on the homosexual activity of the clergy. It must be noted here that homosexuality was not understood then as it is now in the secular world. Historically, homosexuality would have been seen either as a choice made by individuals to behave contrary to 'nature', or as being in some way 'disordered'. Through listening to, and reading the experiences of gay, lesbian, bisexual and trans-gendered people, we have been given greater insight into the realities of their lives and the truths of their sexual orientation. One gay priest, James Alison, describes homosexuality as, 'A non-pathological, regularly occurring minority variation in the human condition.' This is as good a general description as any from one who knows the truth of his life as a gay man and as a priest and who lives it authentically. Unfortunately, many religions, including Catholicism, still retain the medieval outlook on homosexuality, despite the evidence of biology and psychology and the lived experience of people with a same-sex orientation.

Peter Damian was very exercised by sexually abusive behaviour of clerics. He was especially vitriolic about those who engaged in pederasty. But while his document was mainly about homosexual behaviour, it also included what nowadays we would call abuse of vulnerable people, which he terms 'spiritual sons' and 'spiritual daughters'. The document, which was really a long letter to the pope, was called *The Book of Gomorrah* and did not pull any punches. The language is harsh and uncompromising, with some rather eye-watering descriptions of the problem as he saw it. He was particularly critical of church leaders who either turned a blind eye to what was going on, or who were too ready to excuse the offending cleric on the basis of giving him a chance to repent and change his ways. Peter challenges this attitude, saying:

> Surely this impious piety does not cut off the wound, but adds fuel to the fire. It does not prevent the bitterness of this illicit act when committed, but rather makes way for it to be committed freely.
>
> Damian, *Book of Gomorrah*

He spoke with some authority, for as well as being a monk and cleric, he was also a bishop and a cardinal. His reforming work led him to travel throughout Italy, to Germany and to France. One imagines he was reasonably well-informed about the state of the church in his own time.

Peter's main purpose was reform in the church and to this end, presented his treatise to the pope of the day, Leo IX. In his work of reform, Peter was trying to work out whether or not clerical offenders should be dismissed from their priesthood for engaging in homosexual behaviour. He, himself, was in favour of such action, but was looking for guidance from the pope on the issue. Leo, on the other hand, was inclined to see the issue as the problem of the individual cleric and only those who had a long track-record of objectionable behaviour should be dismissed; others, with proper repentance should be returned to parish ministry. Peter paid particular attention to the effect of the abusing cleric on their victims, the pope focused only on the sinfulness of the clerics and their need to repent. For anyone sufficiently interested in dealing with the problem of clerical sexual abuse there is a paper trail to be followed in the history of the church. As Fr Tom Doyle OP, a canon lawyer, says:

> Clergy sexual abuse of minors and vulnerable adults has occurred from the earliest centuries. It has been known to church authorities and is a predictable but highly unfortunate feature of clerical life. It has been denied and hidden by bishops and popes who have consistently acted in a conspiratorial manner to prevent instances of abuse from becoming publicly known, especially to law-enforcement authorities.
>
> Doyle, et al., *Sex, Priests and Secret Codes*, p. 64

It is worth noting here that Fr Doyle was treated very badly by the church authorities because of his advocacy for the abused. However, it is heartening to note that the gospel values of justice and compassion appear to be his driving force, rather than personal advancement.

So the problem of clerical sexual abuse is not new in the church. It would appear to be deeply rooted within its structures. This is not to say that it is widespread or endemic to priesthood. It is a fact that the majority of priests are not abusers. It is a sobering thought to know that a child is more likely to suffer sexual abuse in the home from a family member or close friend of the family, than anywhere else or by anyone else.

The recognised rate of clerical abusers varies from between two and four per cent, depending on the organisation estimating. That means that between ninety-six and ninety-eight per cent have not abused. This is not to minimise the effect of abuse, it is merely to state a fact. This does not mean that all the other ninety-six to ninety-eight per cent behaved impeccably, for included in that figure are all those who knew about, and covered up for, these abusers. Statistically, they might not increase the figure by much, but the extent of the damage they allowed to happen is breathtaking, evidenced by the various reports and accounts of what happened in dioceses around the world. Also, it needs to be acknowledged that abusers tend to have abused multiple children or minors. So to speak of *only* two to four per cent of clerics being abusers is not a negligible statistic.

The fact of clerical sexual abuse within the Catholic Church needs to be faced squarely by all its members. There is a certain tendency with some members of the church to think that once the word 'sorry' has been uttered, even if it took a long time to hear it, there is little more to be said. Also, among those who think this way, there is a tendency to shift the conversation to 'good priests' when the issue of clerical child sexual abuse is raised. Good priests need neither our sympathy nor our understanding because they are 'good'. That is the minimum requirement for the job. What they certainly need is our support and solidarity – that is without argument. But they do not need our sympathy. They ought to have been in the forefront of the righteous indignation when the true scale of the sexual abuse scandal first became evident. But, apart from the few exceptions – the usual suspects, as it were – the silence from priests as a body in the public space was deafening. Before anybody offers an opinion on the motives of survivors of abuse in their search for justice, it is advisable that they take the time to read the various reports issued on clerical sexual abuse in Ireland – all of which are written in clear, accessible language. A particularly instructive document is volume III of what has become known as the Ryan Report into institutional abuse (the formal name is the Commission to Inquire into Child Abuse Report. It is available in many public libraries).

For those who have difficulty acknowledging the reality of clerical sexual abuse, there is a tendency to see the sexual abuse problem as somehow 'new'. As we have seen above, it is not new. It is just more widely known about. When the Catholic Church was the dominant political/ecclesial force in western Europe issues such as the sexual behaviour of priests were conducted more openly through discussions at councils and synods. However, as Catholicism lost its universal hold, such matters became more and more shrouded in secrecy. The stories were kept 'within the family' as it were so that the 'opposition' would not have any ammunition to use. With the development of psychiatry during the twentieth century, the secret of sexual behaviour of priests, especially related to the abuse of children and minors, left the 'family' and became more widely known in the domain of psychiatrists and psychologists. One priest, Fr Gerald Fitzgerald, who had set up a treatment centre for 'troubled' priests, writing to a bishop in 1952 about a particular priest, notes:

> We find it quite common, almost universal with the handful of men we have seen in the last five years who have been under similar charges (abusing children and minors) – we find it quite universal that they seem to be lacking in appreciation of the serious situation … Moreover, in practice, real conversions will be found to be extremely rare. Many bishops believe men are never free from the approximate danger once they have begun. Hence, leaving them on duty or wandering from diocese to diocese is contributing to scandal.
>
> Letter printed in full in Doyle, et al.,
Sex, Priests and Secret Codes

In the early 1950s a Jesuit, Fr William Bier, suggested that candidates for the priesthood should be psychologically screened to avoid accepting people likely to be problematic. It is interesting to note that in Ireland as early as mid-1960s, Fr Seán Fagan, a Marist priest, introduced psychological tests for candidates for priesthood. At that time he was superior of the Marist house of studies and responsible for the young men training for priesthood. This is the same Fr Seán Fagan who was recently silenced by the Vatican department for dogma and doctrine (CDF) after his sixty years of loyal service to the Catholic Church.

What should be clear from all the above is that for anyone in authority who declared that they did not realise the depth or scope of the problem, their ignorance is no defence. The information was available to anybody within the circle who really wanted to know. The question that arises then is: did bishops talk to one another? When the issue of abuse arose in a particular diocese, did that bishop bring his worries and concerns to the meetings of the episcopal conference (the group of bishops in any country or geographical region who meet regularly), and speak to his brother bishops about it? Or when it became known that there was an abusing priest, did his bishop speak frankly to his brothers about the extent of the abuse and the damage it caused? Or did that stereotypical male reflex of not asking for help, not looking for direction, kick in? If so, where does that behaviour fit in with truth and justice that is meant to be the foundation of our Catholic faith?

These questions are important because, in the Irish context, efficient episcopal group action was possible in two instances relating to clerical sexual abuse. The first was that the Irish episcopal conference was able to arrange insurance to cover possible claims arising from clerical sexual abuse as far back as 1987, many years before the depth and breadth of the issue became public knowledge. The second was the removal of Fr Kevin Hegarty from his editorship of the liturgical and pastoral resource magazine, *Intercom*. *Intercom* is published by Veritas which is owned by the Irish bishops. In

March 1994 Fr Hegarty published an article by a Limerick social worker (Philip Mortell) on the impending disaster for the church because of clerical sexual abuse – this was long before the Brendan Smyth exposé which brought the clerical sexual abuse scandal into the public domain. The speed with which Kevin Hegarty was removed from his job and dispatched to a small rural parish in west Mayo was extraordinary. This efficiency of action is thrown into high-relief when compared with the inactions of a number of bishops as shown up in the various reports into clerical child sexual abuse.

Even though clerical sexual abuse of children and its cover-up by bishops is the issue that has rocked the church in a way that has not happened since Luther split with Rome, it is not the only type of sexual abuse. There is also a history of the seduction of emotionally vulnerable adult women who came to their priests needing help and guidance. Peter Damian mentions this briefly in his treatise also. However, there is another type of sexual abuse that has been going on in the church in recent times that has received much less publicity.

In 1994 there was a report submitted to the Vatican by a senior missionary sister in Africa, Sr Maura O'Donoghue, a Medical Missionary of Mary and medical doctor. Through her work with AIDS, Sr O'Donoghue discovered and was deeply shocked by the scale of clerical abuse of a disturbing number of African nuns by some African priests. In her report she laid bare the extent of the abuse. Priests at risk of catching AIDS from prostitutes increasingly began to prey on nuns in convents. Candidates for religious life needed recommendations from their parishes for acceptance into convents. Some were forced to provide sexual favours, and in some cases were raped by the priests they approached for the recommendations. Sr O'Donoghue also noted that some priests encouraged nuns, who had become pregnant by them, to have abortions. She also noted that at least one congregation had to dismiss more than twenty sisters because of pregnancy. In many cases the fathers were priests. It was also noted in the report that women who became pregnant and were dismissed from convents could not go back to their families because of the shame. Penniless, they often ended up in prostitution because they were destitute. The priests involved were allowed remain in ministry. In some cases, they were sent away for a short retreat to think about their behaviour.

One religious superior general of a diocesan congregation complained to her archbishop that twenty-nine of her sisters became pregnant by priests in the diocese. The archbishop dismissed her and illegally appointed another superior general in her place. He had no authority to do this, but that did not prevent him doing it anyway. The deposed superior general appealed to the papal nuncio, Rome's representative in the country, but to no avail. The report continues with the explanation that the low status, and minimal education, of women in many of these countries means they cannot refuse the command of a man. This is more especially so when that man is a priest. Not only was this report submitted, but in 1995 Sr O'Donoghue made personal representations to the appropriate department in the Vatican. No action was taken.

Three years later in 1998, Sr Marie McDonald, a member of the Missionary Sisters of our Lady of Africa (White Sisters) also submitted a report on the abuse of nuns. Her information came from a variety of diocesan congregations and from the Conference of Major Superiors in Africa, so she was confident of their truth. She listed similar situations to Sr O'Donoghue – abuse, rapes, pregnancies, abortions. She also raised the issue at a meeting of African bishops in March 1998. But the bishops did not want to hear about the abuse and implied that the sisters were 'disloyal' to have sent reports outside of their own dioceses. The same conspiracy of silence existed that is a feature of clerical sexual abuse no matter where it occurs.

Despite the provision of these two reports to the Vatican from reputable women, nothing happened on the issue. Though these reports mainly concerned Africa, they refer to a total of twenty-three countries worldwide where similar abuse is taking place. This abuse did not become public knowledge until early 2001, when news of the reports appeared in the *National Catholic Reporter*, a reputable, lay run, Catholic newspaper in the US (www.ncronline.org). Even though the sexual abuse of nuns in developing countries received a certain amount of notice at the time, the issue faded from the public domain very quickly. This is quite extraordinary given the seriousness of the issues concerned.

As with the caveat about the number of child-abusing priests above, it is necessary to say that most indigenous priests live their priesthood with integrity. This is not just an African issue or an Asian issue. This is an issue affecting all of the worshipping community – because if we truly are a community, what hurts one should hurt all.

On one level it is not surprising that clerical child sexual abuse has been in the headlines over and above other forms of clerical sexual abuse. The sexual abuse of children is the most horrible of crimes. Yet, it is necessary to view sexual abuse 'in the round' as it were. Abuse is about the exercise of power and control; about dominating others for one's own selfish ends. If we separate out the abuse into various strands, giving different weight to the types of abuse, we do not tackle the core issues that give rise to it. If the evil remains intact at its core, it will simply raise its nasty head again and again.

Once the issue of clerical sexual abuse was uncovered for all to see, the conversation turned to the causes. Many of a very conservative leaning blamed reforms of Vatican II. This thinking goes: 'If people obeyed the rules, none of this would have happened.' This approach ignores the fact that many of those who ended up in the courts were trained in pre-Vatican II seminaries by priests who grew up in the pre-Vatican II church. It also ignores the historical reality that sexual abuse is not a new phenomenon. Because the sexual abuse of nuns in developing countries points to the behaviour of some indigenous priests, the issue is shunted away from the core problem of abuse. It focuses on the implication that priests from cultures other than American or European are incapable of celibacy. This then becomes an issue of racism and colonialism against all indigenous priests – something to kick against with a sense of righteous anger. The focus is then neatly shifted away from the real problem to a manufactured one.

Even thought there are certain common characteristics, the causes of abuse are multi-faceted and complex. The mistake is to blame any single issue. Various responses to clerical abuse pointed to the sexual immaturity of priests, the church's negative attitude to sex in general and homosexuality in particular, celibacy, paedophilia (sexual attraction to prepubescent children of either sex) and what has become known as ephebophilia (sexual attraction to adolescent males) as likely causes. There is even occasional mention of that catch-all 'systems failure'.

Each of these 'causes' has its champion. And each has the person who argues against it. The truth is probably that there is no single cause. All the above have some role, either singly (such as paedophilia) or in various combinations (such as ephebophilia and sexual immaturity). Even though there is a rush to refuse to blame celibacy because of the many priests who manage to live a celibate life with integrity, celibacy is an undeniable part of the mix. The celibacy that goes along with priesthood is not freely chosen, as some would believe. It has been made part of the package. One cannot be a priest without signing up to celibacy – at least in principle. The role of testosterone within the physiology of the male is rarely mentioned, and usually only in the case of chemical castration for paedophiles. There is a discussion to be had on the role and effect of testosterone on male thinking and actions, and the effects of this on celibate life.

There is also a backlash against blaming homosexuality, but it too is part of the mix. This is particularly so where the person is in denial to himself about his orientation. Given Catholicism's presentation of homosexuality, those who internalise this negative image and repress their true selves, can develop very unhealthy attitudes towards sex. Repressed negative emotion, for all that it is unconscious, finds ways to leak out into conscious behaviour, and often in a most unhealthy way. It is true that many homosexual priests understand and accept themselves fully and live lives of integrity. While the issue of homosexuality in priesthood is a topic that needs to be opened up to debate, assigning to it the sole blame for clerical sexual abuse is a grave injustice. A multi-disciplinary, in-depth study by an independent, reputable organisation or institution, with a proven record in the field of research, needs to be undertaken to study the phenomenon of clerical sexual abuse. This could be a strand of a bigger study on child sexual abuse generally, or a study unto itself. The idea of such an examination of the issue is not new. Cardinal Bernardin of Chicago was deeply concerned about the lack of action on the part of the US bishops on the impending scandal. In 1986 he sent a request to the National Conference of Bishops for an in-depth study on priesthood. Bernardin's memorandum was returned to him by the then general secretary of the conference. Apparently, the committee of bishops that dealt with pastoral life agreed that the bishops would do nothing about the issue. Bernardin resubmitted the memorandum at a later time for consideration by the bishops. He received no response at all the second time.

Unfortunately, the Vatican seems to be looking for the easy answer and men of a homosexual orientation are the obvious targets. There are moves afoot to bar homosexual men from becoming candidates for priesthood. Given that in the US it is accepted that approximately fifty per cent of seminarians are gay, it will be interesting to see if the priest 'shortage' will overcome this resistance to gay men. Or will it continue to be a case of 'don't ask, don't tell' to preserve the fiction that existed up to recently.

As with any abuse, the core issue is the abuse of power. The pope and the worldwide college of bishops need to tackle the issue of power and control within their own ruling structures first. These are the same structures that protected abusers and fostered further abuse by them. Until this happens, abuses of various types will continue to have a deep root in the Catholic Church. Until the gospel values of truth and justice rather than esteem in the eyes of the world are its guiding light, abusive behaviour will find shelter there. Blaming and scapegoating openly gay men simply because of their orientation, will not solve any problems, that will just create a new layer of abuse.

If anything positive can be taken from the tragedy of clerical sexual abuse, and the courageous witness of its survivors, it is that the aura of demigod status of clergy, built up over centuries, has been exposed for what it is – a fiction. Clerics have no more special access to God that the rest of humanity. They are not a privileged class of humanity possessing a direct line to God. The Spirit of God is the spark of life within all human beings, all of whom are called in their own way to live lives of integrity and wholeness.

Here I Stand

There is no such thing as a neutral standpoint – a standpoint outside time and culture. We bring the sum of who we are to our world view. We are constantly interpreting through the lens of our cultural conditioning – our rearing, in other words – and what we learn as we grow in knowledge and experience is coloured by this. The more self-aware we are of the influences that made us and continue our formation, the more encompassing and less defensive, our world view is. That said, no matter how self-aware we are, we are not neutral observers. We are deeply enmeshed in the wonderful, challenging, sometimes heart-breaking, often disappointing, but always amazing, enterprise called life.

Early formation
I was born and raised a Catholic, with all the observances and rituals that implies. Yet for all that God mattered in my life, Catholicism was a rather looser concept. From an early age, I managed somehow to keep some space between the place of God in my life and the formal practice of religion. This was not a conscious act. I was not some kind of precocious child-theologian. It was a more instinctive, almost primal, response to the structure of religion as opposed to the reality of my faith. This was so much an unconscious part of me that I have only come to recognise it now that I am an adult. Part of the explanation for this space between religion and God most likely arises from the fact that I have always been a questioning person. I always needed to know the 'why' of things. It is not that I rejected

things if I did not understand them. It was more a case of putting things on hold until such time as the explanations became clear. Also, I was fortunate not to be a fearful child. I certainly experienced fear at different times and remember the unpleasant feelings associated with it, but I was not, at heart, a fearful person. So the fear that many associate with religion was never my experience.

In growing to maturity, I learned many lessons, about myself and other people. I learned from my own mistakes – and from the mistakes of others, which is a lot less painful! Yet my experience of Catholicism did not really grow in the same way that my experience of life grew. Intellectually and spiritually it was stuck in a sort of juvenile space. I had moved on, but my knowledge and under-standing of Catholicism did not progress beyond what I had learned at school – it was still on hold. As I experienced the challenges, joys, hurts and disappointments of life, Catholicism seemed to speak less and less to it. And the chasm between faith and religious practice widened. Yet, I did not turn my back on it. This was mainly because I now had two children and did not want to deprive them of a spiritual dimension to their lives. It was more about parenting than any personal conviction. Yet, there remained what might be called a small niggle of unease, a tiny pebble in my shoe – able to be ignored, occasionally forgotten about, but would make its presence felt, when I read or heard something that just did not fit with my experience of God.

Vocabulary as empowerment

Part of dealing with any experience is having the right vocabulary – we need the words to be able to express ourselves. My alienation from church was more a sense of something I felt rather than something that I could clearly put into words. This lack of ability to articulate was a barrier to an adult connection with Catholicism. The feeling I remember most is a sense of being on the outside, looking on, knowing that somehow I just did not fit. What contributed to the sense of isolation was that no one in my family and social circle at the time seemed to share my experience of distance and discomfort. Yet my faith in God and the sense of the presence of God in my life never waned through all this.

Over time the practice of my faith through Catholicism no longer seemed to make any sense to me. By now my teenage children had decided for themselves that Catholicism held nothing for them, so I was preparing to make my own break with it. Then, just as I was approaching forty – the great age for taking stock of where you are and what your life is offering – Providence smiled on me. I was fortunate to meet with an Irish theologian Fr Seán Fagan, a Marist priest. Seán had written a bestseller in the 1970s called *Has Sin Changed?* It was a groundbreaking book, and it still finds resonance for people of a certain age. Through Seán, the world of theology was opened up to me, and suddenly my questions found answers. It was like finding a cool spring to drink from after a long, hard trek across a desert. Needless to say, for every question that was answered, two more sprung up in its place. I was, by turns, thrilled beyond words at the riches before me, and hopping mad at what had been offered to me as Catholic throughout my life. To express it biblically, my experience of Catholicism up to then had been a case of looking for bread, but being given stones.

Through Seán's mentoring, I was given bread aplenty – a true feast. It was the best possible theological grounding before any formal studies began. It meant that I took no aspect of theology at face value. I realised that the phrase 'church teaching', a staple of my Catholicism, is a very ambiguous term. Who or what is 'church'? Whose cultural milieu is setting the agenda for the 'teaching'? Who has the competence to teach? Do the teachers understand that life is an evolving process not a series of philosophical propositions? Do the teachers themselves believe they have anything to learn? To whom do the teachers listen – if they listen at all? The questions exploded! But now I had words. Now I knew how to put shape on my feelings and intuitions and bring them forward in new questions. I bounced everything against my experience, realising that theology must speak to practical life if it is to have any value. Ivory-tower theology may be immensely satisfying intellectually (and it is – I can attest to that!), but if it does not find a grounding in the reality of people's lives, it is largely irrelevant, as are its practitioners. I say this even though I find the academic study intensely satisfying ... thrilling, almost!

Formal study of theology
Again Providence smiled. It seemed as if I needed to serve a long apprenticeship of alienation before I was ready for the formal study of theology. Of course, geography was a problem, anchored as I am in the Irish midlands, there was no opportunity to study formally. In 2001 the Irish Dominicans set up a distance education programme to offer a high-quality theological education by distance learning. This was a wonderful initiative by the Dominicans and has served the church well in making theology available to everyone, no matter where they lived. Since 2010, 226 people have graduated with a higher-level qualification in theology, including 70 who were awarded degrees.

The intuitions of my childhood were affirmed and expanded by my experience of doing theology – God was one thing, organised religion, another – they are not same thing. It was a revelation to discover that Greek philosophy has had a far greater influence in the formation of Catholicism, as we know it, than scripture. There were many other such awakenings in my education that all acted as a collective spiritual sigh that said, 'At last! Now it all makes sense. Now the pieces fit.' But this was not the end of the journey. It was just one more step along the way.

The study of theology brought me into contact with many wonderful people. Some were very involved in their parishes, others, like me, were struggling to belong, but felt very much like outsiders. Also, there was a disturbing pattern where the more empowered some people became the more they seemed to be feared by their priests. Apart from those I know through my studies, I also meet an ever-increasing number of people who identify themselves with the excluded as Catholics. This is a slow but steady movement. One of the theologians currently silenced by the Vatican, Fr Owen O'Sullivan, aptly named it 'the silent schism' as far back as 1997. There is a marked reluctance in the church leadership to acknowledge this exodus of Catholics as a symptom of something quite wrong at the heart of Catholicism's own administration. It is much more comfortable to label it individualism, materialism or secularism or any other convenient 'ism'. It is much easier to point a finger and accuse the other than to examine oneself – it is so much easier to be the victim. Even though the move away from church had begun before the scandal of clerical sexual abuse was uncovered, it has significantly influenced the exodus. Even though the abuse perpetrated on children was unspeakable, people are even more horrified at the systematic cover-up by bishops. This damage to church will reverberate for decades to come. Unfortunately, this reality is not appreciated by the most senior levels of the church administration. I thought it bordering on the obscene at the height of the revelations about the extent of clerical sexual abuse worldwide that the Vatican instituted the Year of the Priest. It is understandable that the majority of priests who live good and decent lives felt battered and bruised by the extent of the sexual abuse carried out by their brother priests. It is understandable that many would feel tainted, though they had no reason to feel that way. But that was nothing compared to the sense of betrayal by the church at large. I recall a friend telling me that her father, a devout Catholic all his life who attended daily Mass, did not want a priest to attend him in his final illness. For anyone who understands what we might call 'old-fashioned' Catholicism, that man's refusal to have a priest attend him in his final days was a profound act. But it speaks to the devastating effects of the revelations.

Apologies – too little, too late

Following on from the revelations, the reluctance of the church leaders to apologise properly only added salt to the wound. It took too long for 'official' apologies to be offered to survivors of abuse. One suspects that only the relentless spotlight of the media eventually shamed some leaders into apologies that seemed more akin to sound-byte than something necessarily born from shame and repentance. I believe that a very valuable moment for reconciliation was lost, when legal considerations rather than the imperative of the gospel influenced the hierarchy. The truth of this was brought home in a very personal way some weeks after the feast of St Blaise two years ago.

Once a month, a community of religious, whose chapel I attend for quiet prayer, has a Mass for priests. Occasionally, I catch the end of a Mass when it overlaps with my regular time in the chapel. On the feast of St Blaise, the invited celebrant was performing the usual blessing of the throats, and almost all of the very small congregation went forward for it. Two people, another woman and I, remained in our seats. My own reasons for abstention were theological. I am convinced of the necessity for adults to move on from practices that border on the magical to a mature grasp of faith. So, when the priest looked down expectantly at the pair of dissenting women, I gave a discreet but definite shake of my head indicating my refusal. As I saw him stride determinedly towards me, not only did I shake my head more vigorously, I also raised my hand, palm outward, in the universally understood sign for 'Stop!' Looking somewhat shocked at the refusal, he adjusted course and tacked to my left to where the other woman sat and forced the ritual on her. Assuming that my very clear message had been received and understood, I closed my eyes – a natural act during prayer. Suddenly, I felt his large, heavy hand dropped on my head and the pair of crossed candles pushed under my chin. Although his action would not be prosecutable under civil law, my bodily integrity felt violated. Though there was no physical harm done, I found it an intensely unpleasant experience. It was a disturbing manifestation of a mindset that believes when a woman says 'no', she really means 'yes'. I was very angry, but in deference to the other worshippers, I refrained from slapping his hands away. I did not feel any need to bring it to the attention of the community, and within a very short time I had consigned this ill-mannered, loutish behaviour to oblivion.

Then came the unexpected phone call from the community leader. To hear, out of the blue, the words 'I want to apologise … I am so sorry …' was quite a surprise. What amazed me, though, was the effect of the apology on me. I was profoundly grateful for her acknowledgement of the unacceptable aggressive behaviour of the priest, and her unwillingness to excuse it at any level. What was most interesting was that even though this woman had not personally harmed me, her apology filled my heart. Even though she had not hurt me, she, as a leader, took corporate responsibility for something that happened on her watch. She did this with generosity, graciousness and a lack of equivocation. She had not waited to see if I would complain. There were no 'ifs' no 'buts' no excuses. It was sincere repentance offered with a generous heart. By its spontaneous offering as a response to an injustice, it became so much more than an apology. This is what I found so extraordinary – it was no longer something due to me by right or good manners. It was transformed into total gift to me. It was truly a grace-filled moment – a Eucharistic moment, the enrichment of which I still experience whenever I think of it. Intellectually, I have always understood the importance of the corporate apology, but it was only through my experience I fully appreciated the depth of its meaning.

When one thinks of the utterly insignificant nature of my experience compared to those wounded by abuse, then the importance of the corporate apology to those whose lives have been blighted by clerical sexual abuse takes on a meaning way beyond the words 'I am sorry'. Because the church's corporate 'sorry' had to be dragged through gritted teeth, as it were, its potential as a healing gift to the wounded was lost forever. And even still, there is not a full acceptance among some church members, both lay and clerical, about why survivors of clerical sexual abuse chose to go public. The only answer possible to give to such people is: read the various reports into clerical and institutional abuse. Without reading the reports nobody is equipped to make any comment about survivors, or their motives for going public.

The 'institutional church' is a phrase that is well-known in theological circles, but came into general discussion throughout the years of the uncovering of clerical sexual abuse. For all the negativity expressed about the institutional church, structure is a necessity. It is not possible to have a community of people without having some structure. Rather than the institution itself being the problem, the issue is whether the institution operates with justice and fairness.

Disturbing epiphany

I had an interesting epiphany about ten years ago. On holidays, I read *To the Edge of the Sky*, by Anhua Gao. This was a straightforward narrative of one family's experience living in communist China. Unremarkable, one might think, as there were several in the genre published around the same time. What was most disturbing however, were the parallels I found myself drawing between the totalitarianism of the Chinese government and the institutional structure of my church:

- There were rigid rules, some nonsensical, from which no deviation was allowed.

- Decisions that seriously impinged on people's welfare were made without consultation with those most affected.

- There was discouragement of independent, mature, adult reflection, and those who spoke their minds found that punishment was inevitable and sometimes quite devastating.

- Anonymous denunciations were acted upon and the accused did not get the chance to face their accusers.

- Discussion, consultation or dialogue which by definition, includes a willingness to listen, were alien concepts.

- 'Banishment' to a location or a type of work that was stressful for the accused was a frequent punishment.

Each of the comparisons above have been borne out in my reading of past and contemporary church history and also by listening to the experience of those who have come up against the monolith of church leadership and have the wounds to show for it. When reading church history one realises that, truly, there is nothing new under the sun. The current crisis of emptying churches in the Catholic Church is just one more in a history of crises – but a significant one in that a better-educated laity will not be easily won back. The wrath of God has less meaning for them than the mercy of God.

In her book *Transforming Knowledge*, Elizabeth Minnich speaks of dominant groups who define others by reference to themselves. She says: 'It is simply, that while the majority of humankind was excluded from education and the making of what has been called knowledge, the dominant few not only defined themselves as the inclusive kind of human, but also the norm and the ideal.' By doing this, dominant groups created fundamental definitions of what it means to be human. They had the power to describe and define the norm. This made it difficult for them to think positively about anyone other than themselves, and made them less likely 'to think honestly about the defining few' (pp. 37–8). The hierarchical church falls into this category of a dominant group defining others, and definitely has problems thinking honestly about itself. If those who comprise an organisation cannot think honestly about themselves and their organisation, its structures will be flawed because the primary concern will be the protection of the institution. Unfortunately for those affected by clerical sexual abuse, the church leadership showed just to what extent it was prepared to go to protect itself at the expense of the heart of the Christian message of justice and care for the broken and downtrodden.

Change

Is institutional change possible? Of course it is, because the institution is not some uncontrollable robot – it is made up of people who will choose either to behave well or to behave badly, or who will sit on the fence. If enough people decide to behave justly and fairly, the institution will be fair and just. Pope Francis, with his dismissal of privilege, made a good start with his election in 2013. However, to think in terms of institution is to miss the point of the Christian community. The church is meant to be clusters of smaller communities relating to each other and the world through the gospel. The universality of the church is the common willingness to engage with the message of Jesus – not a monolithic institution having a monarch at its head, and a semi-feudal system of hierarchical layers and unthinking conformity. The structure needs to be local and small. It needs to be inclusive and democratic in its structures. It will not always work perfectly, but it will work. Its success will depend on how it empowers people to grow in and through communion.

This is not a new idea. In Latin America 'basic ecclesial com-munities' were very effective in bringing the gospel to people's everyday lives in 1970s and 1980s. These were small groups in a local community who came together to contemplate the gospel and understand their lives in the light of what they read or heard. It did not matter that many were illiterate, they had ears to hear. Sadly, this energising development in church was slowly asphyxiated, as liberation theology was diluted and diminished by John Paul II. His own cultural conditioning left him with a fear of anything that could possibly be interpreted as communism. There were many in power in the church who appeared to be frightened by liberation theology, seeing a Marxist ideology in every turn. Yet when one reads the work of Gustavo Gutierrez, considered to be the 'father' of liberation theology, one cannot but be struck by his reliance on scripture.

There is an interesting exposition of the power of the small group in *Tipping Point* by Malcolm Gladwell – the optimum functioning number is 150 people. This fact is borne out by a study of Anglican church practice in England in 1990s (Richard Brierly, *The Tide is Running Out*) which discovered that no one pastor seems to be able to cope with more than 150 people if they are to do the job properly. The indigenous Anglican Church in Malaysia has used the idea of 'cell church' to extraordinary effect and has grown exponentially; it is estimated that there are in excess of 75 million members of these cell churches. The cell churches are modelled on the concept of the basic ecclesial communities. This throws an interesting perspective on why the Vatican dismantled the structure of liberation theology through sanctions and the appointments of ultraconservative bishops – was it an irrational fear of Marxist ideology or the power of the small group?

Change is possible. All that is required is the recognition that it *is* possible, and will to make it happen. Therein lies the problem. In the church there is the occasional tinkering here and there, but no real desire for fundamental and radical change. This is no surprise. Back in 1962, Desmond Fennell wrote an article for the magazine *Doctrine & Life* (pp. 246–65). It was entitled 'Will the Irish Stay Christian?'. In it, Fennell came to the conclusion that Ireland would not remain a Catholic country. He drew parallels with other European countries, which, by then were shedding their previously dominant Christian influence. Fennel, in theologian-speak, read the 'signs of the times'. This is not clairvoyance, but simply observing what is going on and then applying a bit of intelligent, reflective thinking to those observations to draw conclusions.

In 1962 it was surely unthinkable that Mass attendance and formal faith practice would diminish to the degree it has. Yet the writing was already on the wall, for those who chose to see it. However, complacency and not a little religious arrogance allowed people to be blind and deaf to the possibility of change from outside influences. People began to travel and to be exposed to ways of life other than their own. Television played an important part in the weakening of the propaganda of both church and state. Access to education helped, especially access to third level education. There is no doubt that the clerical child sexual abuse scandals hastened the exodus considerably, but the movement away from church had already begun long before that. Yet, even still, with the hard evidence of empty pews in front of it, the Irish church still refuses, at an institutional level, to read the signs of the times. There are still mumblings and mutterings of secularism, materialism, relativism. It is always easier to blame the other than to look deep into one's own heart and admit a difficult truth – the speck in your eye is much more visible than the log in mine.

Church in post-Catholic communities

So, where to from here? There are groups trying to instigate and participate in reform and renewal in the church. Theologians and other interested groups organise conferences and seminars, attempting to find a way forward. Though the sincerity and passion with which they are approaching the task is admirable, it is my belief that it is a wasted effort. It gives me no pleasure to make this claim, but nevertheless, I believe it to be true. It is an attempt to pour new wine into old wineskins. We need new wineskins into which we may pour our wine of reform and renewal and our love of church. Though Pope Francis is making interesting decisions, renewal cannot be dependent on the personality and convictions of one man. We are all church – our communities are as varied as our many cultures are. Our church will have particular characteristics where it is the dominant religious force, and others where it is a minority church. One size surely does not fit all.

The repeated calls to realise the reforms of Vatican II seem to fall on deaf ears. Although it may seem counter-intuitive, this is probably a good thing. Vatican II's time has passed. Vatican II was the brave attempt to catch up with the twentieth century. Are we to hope that by the middle of the twenty-first century (being optimistic), that its reforms to catch up with the twentieth century just might be realised?

Emerging churches

Cathy Higgins' book, *Churches in Exile: Alternative Models of Church for Ireland in 21st Century* (Columba Press, Dublin, 2013) looks at emerging churches. One model of 'emerging church', is Women-Church, which is worldwide movement of feminist groups and other non-formal women's groups. It started in the US and was formally recognised and given its name at a major conference in Chicago in 1983. It grew out of the issue of the non-ordination of women in Catholicism, but, despite its Catholic beginnings, is not an organised or a denominational group. It is more a loose affiliation of people who are living their faith in a way that speaks more readily to them than the current, patriarchal Christian Church. It is ecumenical and is not concerned about denominational divisions. It focuses primarily on the full participation of women in the sacramental life of the church and its ministry.

A non-denominational emerging church in Ireland is the Vineyard Association of Churches. It has various networks throughout Ireland, and has its roots in evangelical and Pentecostal movements. Authority is not imposed and it is left to individuals as to how much contact with the central authority they wish to have. The main focus is on sharing the vision of the kingdom of God in members' own communities.

The New Monastics are people who choose to live together in community. They live near cities and towns and experience life in and through the experience of marginalised people. Some groups share their financial resources in common. They operate an 'open-door' policy in sharing meals and celebrations. They see hospitality as a way of breaking down hostility.

There are other groups who are not seeking to form a new emerging church, but meeting in pubs, cafes and in other informal centres, such as Ikon in Belfast. They are trying to see how they can live their faith more authentically in the steps of Jesus.

Such movements of renewal do not have to be separated from the institutional model. The Church of Scotland faced the challenge of renewal with courage and vision. Its *Church Without Walls* report of 2001 was a courageous vision for the future of its church.

A different perspective altogether

To hear of the new emergent churches, or existing institutional churches having vision is heartening. Unfortunately, such vision and faith requires a humility that seems to be singularly lacking in the institutional Catholic Church. A vision such as Church of Scotland's Church Without Walls needs a radical shifting of priorities (summarised by Cathy Higgins):

- From church focus to Christ focus.

- From settled church to church as movement.

- From a culture of guilt to a culture of grace.

- From running congregations to building communities.

- From isolation to interdependence.

- From individualism to teamwork.

- From top-down church to upside-down church.

- From centralised resources to development resources.

- From faith as security to faith as risk.

How do we as Catholics find a way to embody such a vision? We do not have a history of learning from others. The narrow vision of 'one true church' and 'outside the church, no salvation' blinkered the view for centuries. Even still, there is a reluctance to accept that we have anything to learn from our sister churches.

One possible answer is to look at church from a completely different perspective, possibly an unimaginable perspective. Many of the names associated with church are replete with meaning and symbolism: Holy Mother, Bride of Christ, Mystical Body of Christ, A Pilgrim People, People of God. Yet, for many people, these names are the antithesis of their experience of church. A name closer to their experience might be Church as Abusive Parent or Church as Abusive Spouse. This idea will be shocking to many faithful Catholics, even shocking to those who are struggling to belong and work for reform. Yet, it might bring us closer to the kind of reform that is needed. No problem can be solved until the fundamental issues are recognised and named. In trying to reshape the concept of church, this might help to understand why reform is so difficult. It needs to be stressed that when one speaks of abuse, it does not automatically mean sexual abuse. Unfortunately, the two words have become almost permanently linked since the exposure of clerical sexual abuse. There are many abusive behaviours other than sexual abuse – bullying is abusive behaviour, physical violence is abusive behaviour, manipulation of people for one's own selfish motives is abusive behaviour. So the concept of abuse needs to be kept broad in scope.

Let us consider the issues involved in abusive behaviour:

- Control
- How control is achieved
- Secrecy
- Denial
- Collusion

Control: That the church leadership is highly controlling is obvious. The centralising of the administration of the church to the Vatican is a reality. The dilution of the role of the bishop in the local community to that of regional manager in a corporation has robbed it of all meaningful leadership roles. When a bishop is called to Rome to account for his actions, especially when it is a case of speaking out against the institution (even with good cause) it is not unlike how a schoolboy is treated when brought to the Principal's office, it can be that intimidating.

Control is achieved by silencing all serious criticism and opposition. Even the mechanisms that exist for dealing with issues of dissent are highly controlled. The Vatican authorities are judge, jury and executioner in such cases where a theologian is called in. Its methods for dealing with such cases fall far short of international best practice. Another method of control is emotional blackmail. Where a theologian is a member of a religious order or congregation, the pressure is applied to the leader of the congregation or order, to bring the accused person under control. When one understands the dynamics of the religious communities, such pressure is very effective, but hardly ever obvious to outsiders. Control can also be achieved in blocking appointments to pontifical institutes (third level colleges given a teaching mandate from Rome). One of the most petty instances I have heard of a blocking action was when an honorary doctorate was refused to an internationally acknowledged scholar. The pontifical institute where he taught wished to honour his contribution to his field of study over the fifty years of his priesthood. This man's crime? He had spoken positively about women's ordination, and for that, an honorary award that would add nothing to his list of earned qualifications was blocked by the Vatican.

Secrecy: It seems that secrecy is soaked into the very DNA of the church structure; secrecy over critically important and serious matters such as clerical child sexual abuse, and in other less important matters. The church's secrecy on the sexual abuse scandals is widely known by now. There is the secrecy of delations – this is where somebody makes a report (often anonymously) to the Vatican about the activities of a priest or a bishop – it would usually be about something they said publicly, either in preaching or in a statement for comment in the media. The topics most likely to bring a reaction is to speak against the church's ban on various methods of contraception, women's ordination, criticising the church leadership's handling of clerical child sexual abuse when reported to it. Some of these delations are a result of statements made in the public forum, and others are for statements made in closed forums, such as lectures and seminars to specific groups. There are people who pretend to subscribe to the aims of particular groups, but in truth are there to secretly spy and report back on what they perceive as dissident behaviour.

Denial: One of the most powerful self-defence tools is denial. The very nature of denial is that people cannot recognise it in themselves, this is especially so in those engaging in abusive behaviour. The problem, as they see it, is always someone else's fault. Again, sadly, the issue of clerical sexual abuse shows the extent to which the church leadership exercised the self-defence mechanism of denial. Despite the amount of public statements of regret and contrition that have been made, institutional denial is really very deep-rooted. There are still people, both clerical and lay, who do not truly accept the awful reality of clerical sexual abuse. While they accept that it has happened, there are still some who see it primarily as 'the media' trying to damage the church. The sexual abuse problem is seen as something to 'get past' and consign to history, rather than a symptom of something gone terribly wrong in the very structure of the church itself.

Collusion: This is a very uncomfortable topic to discuss in terms of reform. Nobody would like to think of themselves as colluding with unacceptable behaviour – yet it happens all the time, in all kinds of environments. It happens at home, in work, in schools, in recreational clubs and societies. One of the most obvious examples of collusion is where a battered spouse (wife or husband) colludes with the abuser, without realising what it is they are doing, when they always find an excuse for the behaviour. There are many people still actively involved in their church who see that it falls very far short of what it might be. I know so many good people, who disagree with the church on many issues, yet because of their faith stay involved. They understand themselves to be contributing towards a better way of doing things. It also helps to give meaning to themselves as persons with a sense of purpose and focus. Their motives are true, honourable and admirable. Yet, through their support, they continue to shore up an organisation that they know to be unjust in many respects – its attitude to full participation of women, to people in second relationships, to committed lesbian and gay couples, to poor women in developing countries by depriving them of dependable methods of birth control, to mention just a few. A reason for this participation is usually because of a separation of thought between the local priest and 'Rome'. There is often a great relationship in the local parish between priest and the people who still practise. However, this separation does not make sense because when it comes to the crunch, the institution will always win out. It has the power because it makes the rules, it makes the laws, it polices the laws, it controls its courts, it hands down the punishment. For as long as it sees no profit in change, it will not change.

People power – a reality in church
When challenged about colluding and enabling destructive behaviour, people still involved cannot see a way through. There is often a fatalistic 'what can we do?' attitude. Due to the fact that the majority of the members of church are excluded from any decision-making in church, there is a perception that we are helpless. But this does not have to be so. Working for change and reform in church can be viewed as David facing Goliath, and therein lies the means for change. We cannot fight Goliath on Goliath's terms. Like David, we need to shed the armour more suited to our opponent – it is an encumbrance; it is weighing us down. We need to use the stones in our slingshots: our education, our determination, our imagination,

the immense possibilities of computer technology and our willingness to act decisively on a small scale. It can be done. The question is: are we willing? Have we the courage of our convictions?

Such willingness and courage requires a deep searching about one's motives and one's true hope for the future of the church. Then it would require a determination to see it through. The means to challenge the unjust structures of the church is one that is applied in many situations where there is destructive, addictive behaviour – detach with love.

To detach with love is not to abandon everything. It is to see the problem, name it and hand it back: 'This is a problem of your making, not mine. I cannot help you. You must help yourself by making necessary changes.' This detachment requires determination and self-discipline, and is difficult and at times painful, but it is possible. If all those people who truly believe that change is necessary decided to detach, it is possible that change might happen. If particular behaviour is enabled, there is no impetus to change it. Waiting for change in church will be a wait in vain. It is not enough to say that change comes slowly, when those who work for change are punished and silenced. Change cannot happen in those circumstances – the Spirit is stifled by the need to control.

When one detaches with love, the door is left open for return when the necessary changes are made and a willingness to change clear. To detach with love is not to be without community. It can be the impetus to create small communities that, in the end, will be the oxygen for the church of the future, if it is to have a life. So even though we are excluded from influence because of the refusal of the church to allow us full participation, we have far more power than we realise. The question remains, have we the courage and vision to use it?

Jesus did not offer certainty and comfort to his followers nor to us. He offered the challenge to think for ourselves, to question our motives and to act with justice. His mission was constantly looking outwards – how are we treating those who are disadvantaged in some way? How are we behaving in our day-to-day dealing with others – are we fair, honest and just? How are we dealing with those who are not part of our 'tribe'? Jesus continually challenged complacency, comfort and the safe option. He continually asked the awkward question, made the awkward challenge. We hear much about Jesus' message being one of love, and it was, but not a warm, fuzzy, cosy love. Jesus constantly showed love through justice, which is altogether more challenging and deeply uncomfortable, if we truly engage with it.

If someone said to us, as in Yann Martel's *Life of Pi*: 'I know what you want. You want a story that won't surprise you. That will confirm what you already know. That won't make you see higher or further or differently. You want a flat story. An immobile story. You want a dry, yeastless, factuality.' Can we deny this accusation? If we say we want reform but collude and enable the behaviour that makes reform impossible, what kind of a Christian story do we truly want?

Bibliography

Alberigo, Giuseppe, gen. ed., and Joseph Komonchak, ed. *History of Vatican II*, 5 vols, Maryknoll, NY: Orbis, 1995–2006. (An excellent history of the event.)

Allen, Horace T., Jnr. 'Common Lectionary and Protestant Hymnody: Unity at the Table of the Word – Liturgical and Ecumenical Bookends' in James F. Puglisi, ed. *Liturgical Renewal as a Way to Christian Unity*, Collegeville, MN: Liturgical Press (a Pueblo book), 2005.

Beal, John P., et al., eds. *New Commentary on the Code of Canon Law*, Mahwah, NJ: Paulist Press, 2000.

Benedict XVI. *Pastoral Letter of the Holy Father Benedict XVI to the Catholics of Ireland*, March 2010, available at: <http://www.vatican.va/holy_father/benedict_xvi/letters/2010/documents/hf_ben-xvi_let_20100319_church-ireland_en.html>

Bermejo, Luis M., SJ. *Infallibility on Trial: Church, Conciliarity and Communion*, Westminster, MD: Christian Classics, 1992.

Bokenkotter, Thomas. *A Concise History of the Catholic Church*, New York: Doubleday, 2004.

Bradshaw, Paul F. *Eucharistic Origins*, London: SPCK, 2004.

Brierly, Richard. *The Tide is Running Out: What the English Church Attendance Study Reveals*, London: Christian Research, 2000.

Brown Raymond E., et al., eds. *The New Jerome Biblical Commentary*, London: Geoffrey Chapman 1989.

Byrne, Lavinia. *Woman at the Altar*: *The Ordination of Women in the Roman Catholic Church*, London: Mowbray, 1994.

Chadwick, Henry. *The Church in Ancient Society: From Galilee to Gregory the Great*, Oxford: OUP, 2001.

Chaves, Mark. *Ordaining Women: Culture and Conflict in Religious Organisations*, Cambridge, MASS: Harvard University Press, 1997.

Code of Canon Law, with index, trans. by Canon Law Society of Great Britain and Ireland, London: Collins Liturgical Publications, 1983.

'*Comme le Prevoit*: On the Translation of Liturgical Texts for Celebrations with a Congregation', available at: <http://www.ewtn.com/library/CURIA/CONSLEPR.HTM>

Congar, Yves, OP. *Tradition and Traditions: An Historical and a Theological Essay*, trans. Michael Nasebury & Thomas Rainborough, London: Burns & Oates, 1963.

Coriden, James, et al. *The Art of Interpretation: Selected Studies on the Interpretation of Canon Law*, Washington, DC: Canon Law Society of America, 1982.

Cozzens, Donald. *Faith that Dares to Speak*, Collegeville, MN: Liturgical Press, 2004.

Crossan, John Dominic. *In Search of Paul: How Jesus' Apostle Opposed Rome's Empire with God's Kingdom*, New York: HarperSanFrancisco, 2004.

Daly, Gabriel. 'Catholic Fundamentalism', in Angela Hanley & David Smith, eds. *Quench not the Spirit: Theology and Prophecy for the Church in the Modern World*, Dublin: The Columba Press, 2005.

Damian, Peter. *Book of Gomorrah: An Eleventh Century Treatise Against Clerical Homosexual Practices*, trans. Pierre J. Payer, Waterloo, ON: Wilfrid Laurier University Press, 1982.

Davis, Leo Donald. *The First Seven Ecumenical Councils (325–587): Their History and Theology*, Collegeville, MN: The Liturgical Press (A Michael Glazier Book), 1983.

DeBroucker, José, ed. *The Suenens Dossier: The Case for Collegiality*, Dublin: Gill & Macmillan, 1970.

Didache: Or the Teaching of the Twelve Apostles, trans. James A. Kleist SJ, *Ancient Christian Writers: The Works of the Fathers in Translation*, No. 6, Mawah, NJ: Paulist Press, 1948.

Doyle, Thomas et al. *Sex, Priests and Secret Codes: The Catholic Church's 2000-year Paper Trail of Sexual Abuse*, Los Angeles: Volt Press, 2006.

Duffy, Eamon. *Saints & Sinners: A History of the Popes*, New Haven: Yale University Press, 1997.

Dulles, Avery, SJ. *The Craft of Theology: From Symbol to System*, New York: Crossroads, 1995.

Fagan, Sean, SM. *Has Sin Changed?* Dublin: Gill & Macmillan, 1978. Revised and published as *What Happened to Sin?* Dublin: The Columba Press, 2008. As a result of the publication of this 2nd edition, Fr Fagan was censured by the Vatican's Congregation for the Doctrine of the Faith. He was forbidden to write, teach or broadcast. This punishment was to be kept secret under threat of dismissal from the priesthood and his Marist congregation by the CDF. The threat of dismissal was recently withdrawn, but all other sanctions remain in place.

Faivre, Alexandre. *The Emergence of the Laity in the Early Church*, trans. David Smith, Mahwah, NJ: Paulist Press, 1990.

Fennell, Desmond. 'Will the Irish Stay Christian?' *Doctrine & Life*, vol. 12, no. 5 (May 1962) pp. 246–65. Part of this article was republished in *Religious Life Review*, 41:215 (July–August 2002).

Fesquet, Henri. *The Drama of Vatican II: The Ecumenical Council June 1962–December 1965*, trans. Bernard Murchland, New York: Random House, 1967.

Fiedler, Maureen and Linda Rabben, eds. *Rome Has Spoken: A Guide to Forgotten Papal Statements and How They Have Changed Through the Centuries*, New York: Crossroads, 1998.

Fiorenza, Elizabeth. *In Memory of Her: A Feminist Theological Reconstruction of Christian Origins*, London: SCM Press, 1983.

Flannery, Austin, OP, ed. *Vatican Council II, Vol I: Conciliar and Post Conciliar Documents*, Dublin: Dominican Publications, 1998. The documents are also available at: <http://www.ewtn.com/library/councils/v2all.htm>

Freeman, Charles. *A New Early History of Christianity*, New Haven: Yale University Press, 2011.

Freyne, Sean. *Jesus, A Jewish Galilean: A New Reading of the Jesus Story*, London: Continuum, 2004.

Gaillardetz, Richard R. *The Church in the Making: Lumen Gentium, Christus Dominus, Orientalium Ecclesiarum (Rediscovering Vatican II)*, Mahwah, NJ: Paulist Press, 2006. (Rediscovering Vatican II is a series of eight books reflecting on the sixteen basic documents of the Council forty years later. The least satisfactory volume is that which includes *Gaudium et Spes*, the document on the church in the modern world, otherwise it is a useful series.)

Gao, Anhua. *To the Edge of the Sky: A Story of Love, Betrayal, Suffering, and the Strength of Human Courage*, New York: Overlook Press, 2003.

Gladwell, Malcolm. *The Tipping Point: How Little Things Can Make a Big Difference*, New York: Little, Brown, 2006.

Hannon, Sr Vincent Emmanuel. *The Question of Women and the Priesthood: Can Women be Admitted to Holy Orders?* London: The Catholic Book Club, 1967.

Häring, Bernard. *Free and Faithful: My Life in the Catholic Church, An Autobiography*, Ligouri, MO: Ligouri Publications, 1998.

Häring, Bernard. *My Witness for the Church*, trans. Leonard Swidler, Mahwah, NJ: Paulist Press, 1992.

Harrington, Wilfrid, OP. *Mark: Realistic Theologian: The Jesus of Mark*, Dublin: The Columba Press, 2002. (There are four books in this series, one for each evangelist.)

Hebblethwaite, Peter. *John XXIII: Pope of the Council*, London: Geoffrey Chapman, 1984.

Higgins, Cathy. *Churches in Exile: Alternative Models of Church for Ireland in 21st Century*, Dublin: The Columba Press, 2013.

Jeffrey, Peter. *Translating Tradition: A Chant Historian Reads Liturgiam Authenticam*, Collegeville, MN: Liturgical Press (a Pueblo Book), 2005.

Kaiser, Robert Blair. *The Pope, Council and World: The Story of Vatican II*, New York: Macmillan, 1963.

Kelly, J. N. D. *Early Christian Creeds*, London: Continuum, 2006.

Kelly, Joseph F. *The Ecumenical Councils of the Catholic Church: A History*, Collegeville, MN: The Liturgical Press (A Michael Glazier Book), 2009.

Kerr, Ian and Terrence Merrigan, eds. *The Cambridge Companion to John Henry Newman*, Cambridge: CUP, 2009.

Komonchak, Joseph, et al., eds. *The New Dictionary of Theology*, Collegeville, MN: The Liturgical Press (A Michael Glazier Book), 1987.

Küng, Hans. *Structures of the Church*, New York: Thomas Nelson, 1964.

LaCugna, Catherine Mowry, ed. *Freeing Theology: The Essentials of Theology in Feminist Perspective*, New York: HarperCollins, 1992.

Latourelle, Rene and Rino Fisichella, eds. *Dictionary of Fundamental Theology*, New York: Crossroads, 1994.

Leo XIII. *Rerum Novarum* (encyclical of Pope Leo XIII on capital and labour), May 1891, available at: <http://www.vatican.va/holy_father/leo_xiii/encyclicals/documents/hf_l-xiii_enc_15051891_rerum-novarum_en.html>

Leo XIII. *Providentissimus Deus* (encyclical of Pope Leo XIII on the study of holy scripture), November 1893, available at: <http://www.vatican.va/holy_father/leo_xiii/encyclicals/documents/hf_l-xiii_enc_18111893_providentissimus-deus_en.html>

Lonergan, Bernard. *Method in Theology*, Toronto: University of Toronto Press, 1973/1999.

Marty, Martin E. and R. Scott Appleby, eds. *Fundamentalisms Observed*, vol I, Chicago: University of Chicago Press, 1994.

McAleese, Mary. *Quo Vadis? Collegiality in the Code of Canon Law*, Dublin: The Columba Press, 2012.

McBrien, Richard P. *The Church: The Evolution of Catholicism*, New York: HarperOne, 2008.

McClory, Robert. *Turning Point: The Inside Story of the Papal Birth Control Commission and How Humanae Vitae Changed the Life of Patty Crowley and the Future of the Church*, New York: Crossroads, 1995.

McGrath, Alister E. *Christian Theology: An Introduction*, Oxford: Blackwell, 1997.

Martell, Yann. *Life of Pi*, Orlando, FL: Harcourt Publishing Co. (A Harvest book), 2001.

Minnich, Elizabeth. *Transforming Knowledge*, Philadelphia, PA: Temple University Press, 2005.

National Catholic Reporter. Available at: <www.ncronline.org> A fortnightly moderate US newspaper of Catholic interest, in print since 1964 – primarily focused on the church in the United States, but includes excellent articles of worldwide interest. It has a substantial searchable archive.

Neuner, Josef, SJ and Heinrich Roos SJ, with Karl Rahner SJ, ed. *The Teaching of the Catholic Church as Contained in Her Documents*, New York: Alba House, 1967.

Neuner, Josef, SJ and Jacques Dupuis SJ. *The Christian Faith in the Doctrinal Documents of the Catholic Church*, London: Collins, 2001.

Newman, John Henry. *On Consulting the Faithful on Matters of Doctrine*, edited with introduction by John Coulson, London: Sheed & Ward, 1961.

Nolan, Albert. *Jesus Before Christianity*, Maryknoll, NY: Obis Books, 1992.

Noonan, John T. *Contraception: A History of Its Treatment by the Catholic Theologians and Canonists*, Cambridge, MASS: Belknap Press (Harvard University Press), 1986.

O'Malley, John W. *What Happened at Vatican II*, Cambridge, MASS: Belknap Press (Harvard University Press), 2008.

O'Sullivan, Owen, OFM Cap. *The Silent Schism: Renewal of Catholic Spirit and Structures*, Dublin: Gill & Macmillan, 1997.

Örsy, Ladislas, SJ. *The Church: Learning and Teaching: Magisterium, Assent, Dissent, Academic Freedom*, Dublin: Dominican Publications, 1987.

Örsy, Ladislas, SJ. 'The Interpretation of Laws: New Variations on an Old Theme', in Coriden, 1982, above.

Paul VI. *Humanae Vitae* (encyclical of Paul VI on the regulation of birth), July 1968, available at: <http://www.vatican.va/holy_father/paul_vi/encyclicals/documents/hf_p-vi_enc_25071968_humanae-vitae_en.html>

Pius X. *Pascendi Dominici Gregis* (encyclical of Pope Pius X on the doctrines of the Modernists), September 1907, available at: <http://www.vatican.va/holy_father/pius_x/encyclicals/documents/hf_p-x_enc_19070908_pascendi-dominici-gregis_en.html>

Pius X. The Holy Roman and Universal Inquisition (now known as the Congregation for the Doctrine of the Faith). *Lamentabili Sane Exitu*, July 1907, available at: <http://www.papalencyclicals.net/Pius10/p10lamen.htm> This document was prepared by the Roman Inquisition but is clearly marked as being 'under Pius X' at the head of the document.

Pius XI. *Casti Conubii* (encyclical of Pope Pius XI on Christian marriage), December 1930, available at: <http://www.vatican.va/holy_father/pius_xi/encyclicals/documents/hf_p-xi_enc_31121930_casti-connubii_en.html>

Pius XII. *Divino Afflante Spiritu* (encyclical of Pope Pius XII on promoting biblical studies), September 1943, available at: <http://www.vatican.va/holy_father/pius_xii/encyclicals/documents/hf_p-xii_enc_30091943_divino-afflante-spiritu_en.html>

Pius XII. *Humani Generis* (encyclical of the Holy Father Pope Pius XII concerning some false opinions threatening to undermine the foundations of Catholic doctrine), August 1950, available at: <http://www.vatican.va/holy_father/pius_xii/encyclicals/documents/hf_p-xii_enc_12081950_humani-generis_en.html>

Quinn, John. *Reform of the Papacy: The Costly Call to Christian Unity*, New York: Herder & Herder, 1999.

Ratzinger/Messori. *The Ratzinger Report: An Exclusive Interview on the State of the Church*, trans. Salvator Attanasio & Graham Harrison, San Francisco: Ignatius Press, 1985.

Runciman, Steven. *The Eastern Schism: A Study of the Papacy and the Eastern Churches During the XIth and XIIth Centuries*, Oxford: Clarendon Press, 1955; special reprint edn, 1997.

Rynne, Xavier. *Letters from Vatican City: Vatican Council II (First Session): Background and Debates*, London: Faber & Faber, 1963.

Rynne, Xavier. *The Second, Third and Fourth Sessions: Debates and Decrees of Vatican Council II*, 3 vols, London: Faber & Faber, 1964–6. (Rynne's work is a contemporaneous account of Vatican II, offering rare insights into the background events.)

Sacrorum Antistitum (*Motu Proprio*) only available in Latin on the Vatican website. An English version is available at: <http://www.papalencyclicals.net/Pius10/p10moath.htm> but this is somewhat sanitised because the introduction is omitted. An English translation of this introduction is available in *The American Ecclesiastical Review*, vol. 143, July–December

1960, pp. 239–40 and gives a clearer idea of the intention behind the Motu Proprio. A PDF version is available at: <http://www.u.arizona.edu/~aversa/modernism/sa.pdf>

Schultenover, David G., ed. *Vatican II: Did Anything Happen?* New York: Continuum, 2007.

Sullivan, Francis, SJ. *Creative Fidelity: Weighing and Interpreting Documents of the Magisterium*, Eugene, OR: Wipf & Stock, 2003 (published by Paulist Press, 1996).

Sullivan, Maureen. *The Road to Vatican II: Key Changes in Theology*, Mahwah, NJ: Paulist Press, 2007.

The Tablet. Available at: <www.thetablet.co.uk> A weekly moderate UK Catholic newspaper, with a broad scope, published continually since 1840. It has a complete, searchable archive online.

Tanner, Norman P., SJ, ed. *Decrees of the Ecumenical Councils*, 2 vols, London: Sheed & Ward, 1990. This contains the full record of the available decrees and canons of the Ecumenical Councils of the church. For some of the earliest Councils, only part of the documentation is available.

Taylor, Maurice. *It's the Eucharist, Thank God*, Brandon, Suffolk: Decani Books, 2006.

Tierney, Brian. *Foundations of the Conciliar Theory: The Contribution of the Medieval Canonists from Gratian to the Great Schism*, Cambridge: CUP, 1973.

Tierney, Brian. *Origins of Papal Infallibility 1150–1350: A Study on the Concepts of Infallibility, Sovereignty and Tradition in the Middle Ages*, Leiden: E. J. Brill, 1972. (Tierney's work is an outstanding example of how scholarly writing does not need to be pedantic and tediously boring.)

Valsecchi, Ambrogio. *Controversy: The Birth Control Debate 1958–1968*, trans. Dorothy White Washington, DC: Corpus Books, 1968.

Witherup, Ronald, *Scripture: Dei Verbum: Rediscovering Vatican II*, New York: Paulist Press, 2006.

Young, Frances. *From Nicaea to Chalcedon: A Guide to the Literature and Its Background*, London: SCM Press, 1983.